COUSIN BRUCIE! MY LIFE IN ROCK 'N' ROLL RADIO

COUSIN BRUCE MORROW
AND
LAURA BAUDO

Introduction by Neil Sedaka

BTB
BEECH TREE BOOKS
WILLIAM MORROW
New York

Grateful acknowledgment is made for permission to reprint from the following:

OH! CAROL by Neil Sedaka and Howard Greenfield. Copyright © 1959, 1960 by Screen Gems-EMI Music Inc. All rights reserved. Used by permission.

HELLO AGAIN by Sunny Skylar and Herb Oscar Anderson. Copyright © 1960, 1962 by SOUTHERN MUSIC PUBLISHING CO., INC. International Copyright Secured. ALL RIGHTS RESERVED. Used by permission.

MONA LISA by Jay Livingston and Ray Evans. Copyright © 1949 by Famous Music Corporation. Copyright renewed 1976 by Famous Music Corporation.

HEY JUDE by John Lennon and Paul McCartney. © 1968 NORTHERN SONGS, LIMITED. All Rights for the U.S., Canada and Mexico Controlled and Administered by BLACKWOOD MUSIC INC. Under License from ATV Music (MACLEN). All Rights Reserved. International Copyright Secured. Used by Permission.

TIME IN A BOTTLE by Jim Croce. © 1971 DenJac Music Company and MCA Music, A Division of MCA Inc., 40 West 57th Street, New York, N.Y. 10019. ALL RIGHTS ADMINISTERED BY DENJAC MUSIC COMPANY. USED BY PERMISSION. ALL RIGHTS RESERVED.

Library of Congress Cataloging-in-Publication Data

Morrow, Cousin Bruce.
  Cousin Brucie!

1. Morrow, Cousin Bruce.   2. Disc jockeys—United States—Biography.   3. Rock music—United States—History and criticism.   I. Baudo, Laura.   II. Title.
ML429.M78A3   1987   791.44'5[B]   87-14328
ISBN 0-688-06615-1

Printed in the United States of America

First Edition

1 2 3 4 5 6 7 8 9 10

BOOK DESIGN BY BRIAN MOLLOY

The word "book" is said to derive from *boka,* or beech.
The beech tree has been the patron tree of writers since ancient times and
represents the flowering of literature and knowledge.

To my mom and dad.
To my children, Jon, Paige, and Meri.
To my best friend, my darling Jodie.

ACKNOWLEDGMENTS

Many people lent their time, energy, advice, support, and spirit to the creation of this book. Though any list brings with it the danger of forgetting someone, that risk had to be taken in order that the following people be remembered:

Perry Bascomb, Ken Belton, Sid Bernstein, Frank Cammarata, Rod Calarco, Clay Cole, Ron Cutler, Joe Dera, Harry Harrison, Dan Ingram, Robert Kipperman, Chuck Leonard, Richard Lorenzo, Ron Lundy, Joe McCoy, Jeff Mazzei, Les Marshak, Frank Murphy, the Museum of Broadcasting, Harry Ploski, Wally Schwartz, Neil Sedaka, David Singer, Rick Sklar, Bob Shannon, Walt Sabo, Jr., and Nancy Widmann, and especially Jodie Morrow.

Laura Baudo would like to extend thanks also to Scott Campbell, Jeanette Garten, Jon H. Roberts and Ethel Romm for their guidance and example, and to Robert Sillerman for the same and much more.

Additional thanks to Arthur and Richard Pine, who got the story to the right publisher, and to James Landis for being the right publisher. Special mention must be made of Jane Cavolina Meara, editor, fan, inspiration, and friend, for unending encouragement and wisdom.

Finally, gratitude to everyone who played a part in the magic that was WABC radio, with particular note of the late Bob Lewis, in hopes that the Divariable Veeblefurtzer has carried him to a great shift in heaven.

CONTENTS

INTRODUCTION

Bruce Morrow and I have been friends since 1959, when I did a record hop for him at a radio station in Miami, Florida. He was a struggling DJ and I a struggling singer/songwriter. I remember how impressed I was when I first met him and his late first wife, Susan. Our lives seemed intertwined from that time on. When Leba and I were first married, we moved into 370 Ocean Parkway in Brooklyn, where, ironically, Bruce and Susan were already living. We started our families at the same time and raised our children together. When Bruce did his live Palisades Park shows, he would frequently invite me to sing. We always took our kids along and, after the show, we would take them on all the rides in the park. I remember the delighted screams of John, Paige, Meri, Dara, and Marc.

As the years went on, it was destined that we Brooklyn boys would continue our closeness. I moved my family to a community called Merriewold Park in upstate New York and convinced the Morrows to buy a home there soon after. What marvelous memories I have of Bruce on his snowmobile in the woods and on the lake. We swam, barbecued, and kibitzed. He even took me to visit his old summer camp. You can imagine the excitement among the campers when Cousin Brucie and Neil Sedaka made an appearance together.

It was great watching Bruce's dreams become reality as he became a top disc jockey in New York City, with a tremendous reputation and following. Who didn't listen to Cousin Brucie on WABC during those golden days of rock 'n' roll? He was talented, clean, sharp, and really cared about the music and the people who made it. His voice and personality were distinctive, filled with warmth and charm, and his enthusiasm and energy were contagious. Listening to Bruce on the air was like listening to an old friend, and the kids related to him as if he really were their cousin. Bruce has a genuine fondness for people and has always gone out of his way to greet his many fans, always making them feel special, never slighting anyone. Bruce and rock 'n' roll are synonymous. He epitomized the whole culture of the times: fun-loving, spontaneous, wonderfully childlike, and carefree.

I've always said the public can't be fooled. Bruce is for real and, in a business as rough as the music industry, it's sometimes hard to believe that a person like him still exists. He has always loved what he does, and that's what sets him apart from all the rest. The new radio people certainly have a lot to learn from Bruce—he's a tough act to follow. There are originals and there are copiers, and Bruce is definitely one of the originals. I'm proud to have watched his success grow, and I say, "Hooray for rock 'n' roll and hooray for Cousin Brucie."

—NEIL SEDAKA

Can't you hear that groovy beat, now baby?
Don't you want to tap your feet, now baby?
Come on, let's go, go, go
What a groovy show
Come on, and go, go, go
With Cousin Brucie.
Go, go. Go, go. Go, go.

Can't you hear that drummer man, now baby?
Don't you want to clap your hands, now baby?
Come on, let's go, go, go
What a groovy show
Come on, and go, go, go
With Cousin Brucie.
Go, go. Go, go. Go, go.

Movin' and a-groovin'
Havin' a ball
With Cousin Brucie
Go, go. Go, go. Go, go.

"The Cousin Brucie Theme Song"
A gift from Frankie Valli and the Four Seasons

PROLOGUE

The 1959 Chevrolet Impala convertible was about the most wonderful car anybody had ever seen. Long, low, with fins like eyebrows arched over the taillights, it was the perfect chariot for the fiery young gods of the early sixties. Take the top down on one of those babies and you had a mean, lean cruising machine. You were out to look and to be seen. Hell, the car was so wide and the couch seats so inviting that three guys could squeeze five girls inside in no time.

On one of those soft summer nights when the air felt like suede, you wanted to ride around forever. At twenty-nine cents for a gallon of high test, you got a night's worth of transportation and freedom for about a buck and a half.

In Lodi, New Jersey, the kids would check out the action at the Wetson's hamburger stand—fifteen cents for a burger, a dime for a Coke. Nobody had called it fast food yet, but things had certainly started to speed up. On Long Island, heavy Chevies, somber Fords, and the occasional sexy 'Vette would sail into Louie's Clam Bar (SHOES AND SHIRTS MUST BE WORN) to see

15

what the action was. In Darien, Connecticut, home of the Villager and Gant shirt set, they piled into expensive foreign sedans and headed for Rowayton Beach. Meanwhile, on the isle of Manhattan, they walked. Kids moved up and down the East and West sides, meandered through midtown, and wandered down to the Village. If they needed to go beyond the bounds of the neighborhood, they could take the bus or the subway, or, if they came from flush Park Avenue or Central Park West, they'd hop into a cab, preferably a Checker with room enough for a crowd inside. All over America, a steady stream of youth was floating on the summer air, going exactly where they wanted to go—no place special.

The boys and girls in Bayside, Queens, didn't know their counterparts in Toms River, New Jersey, or Bel Air, California. Westport could barely imagine Staten Island, let alone Gary, Indiana, yet they were all connected. They were connected by their youth and by a magic machine that had made them the royalty of the country. The nation revered the young and radio was the kingdom that belonged to them.

The kingdom had jesters, town criers, jugglers, entertainers. They were called disc jockeys. And one of them sounded like this:

> "Hello, my friends . . . what a beautiful night to be in love. Your Cousin Brucie is here with the best summer songs of the best summer ever. Tonight we're going to rock, we're going to roll, we're going to do some fast dancin' and we're going to take it real, real slow. Now, hug your baby tight and listen to this new song that's headed straight for the top . . ."

Come with me to August 1963:

Inside the studio, the Ronettes fill my headset with "Be My Baby" in simple monaural sound. I reach for the log and check the next commercial—Dennison's: "Money talks, nobody walks," the copy goes in a bebop rap style. This retailer has the commercials everybody

16

recalls, even if they have no idea what they mean. Ask somebody where to buy a cheap suit and the name Dennison's will surely be the reply. Bop works, is that lesson.

Saul, my engineer, has the Dennison's cartridge cued and ready to ride as soon as the record's over. No cut to Brucie until after the news. I take the headphones off and sit back in the high swivel chair. I don't get up. I rarely leave the studio during a show. Straying too far from the mike will break the spell. Every night is like an upbeat teenage séance. The kids are cruising the Planet Earth. I'm out there in the ionosphere somewhere. The only way to keep contact is to keep them in my mind—to picture them, to know what they're doing, what they look like, how they think, how they sound. I know what makes them happy and what makes them cry. I learn these things when I make personal appearances. At a shopping-center opening, a girl named Mary Anne or Gail or Maria will tell me that her boyfriend's name is Danny or Jack or Luis. He's so boss. He wears Canoe cologne and looks like Dion.

I signal Saul to open my mike. I check my notes. About half an hour ago a girl called to ask me to dedicate a song. It's a typical dedication. Two friends probably talked on the phone for about three hours and dared each other to do it until one got up the courage to call. It's part of the mating ritual of 1963; it's how the young maidens make contact with the braves.

"This song goes out to Bobby and Mike in Rego Park. It's from Patty and June. Oh, you lucky, lucky guys. Here's 'I'm Leavin' It Up to You' by Dale and Grace."

Tomorrow Patty and June will meet for a root beer float. They'll scream when they see each other and say something like this:

"Did you hear it? Cousin Brucie played it! Oh my God, I'm going to die! Do you think they heard it? Oh my God. If Bobby ever calls, I'll die! Oh, God, he's so cute. Oh God, he dresses so great. I'm going to die! If he asks me to the dance next week, I'll die! He played it. You call him next time.

17

PROLOGUE

Ask him to play 'Candy Girl.' Oh God, I'm going to die!''

CUE BRUCIE. OPEN THE MIKE. A LIVE SPOT:

"Hey cousins. I've got some very special things planned for you this Saturday and Sunday live at Palisades Park. The Chiffons . . . the Orlons . . . the Crystals . . . and the summer's hottest star, Lesley Gore! Bring all of your friends, bring Mom, bring Dad. We're going to be giving away records and albums, we'll be dancing, we'll be taking dedications, and everybody is going to have a ball. I promise you a day to remember, my cousins, so be there! And now, a word from our friends at the lovely Public Service Bus Company."

11:10 P.M. Fifty minutes left of a two-hour shift that always seems like two fleeting minutes. The station is quiet now. I like it this way— just me, Saul, and my own private hookup to the world. Rick Sklar, the program manager, isn't around to insert "science" into what is clearly more mystical—the growing popularity of WABC radio. Charlie Greer, who has the shift after mine, isn't in yet. That's no surprise. Charlie is pathologically late. I'm always cuing his first record, making sure his engineer racks up his jingle, and then sitting there waiting to see if after two songs I'll have to take the mike. Two songs and one spot maximum before the mike is open—that's the rule for starting someone else's show. This is personality radio and the listeners expect to hear live people. There are still fifty minutes before I've got to worry about Charlie. Besides, I don't care about staying late. I could live in the studio and be happy as long as I got out for the appearances where I meet the kids.

That's what life was like when I was twenty-seven years old. Heavy Chevies and light hearts were the order of the day. All around the country, the cars, the mood, the very fiber of youthfulness was being synthesized by a phenomenon called

18

rock 'n' roll radio. WABC, New York was about to be recognized as the strongest force in the history of rock radio, and not long after that I would be one of the ratings leaders on that force. Later, I somehow came to stand for the station that stood for the most powerful musical movement ever. Where did the station come from? Where did the music come from? I know a little about that and a lot about where the disc jockey came from, and such is the story I want to tell.

It may be only one man's story, and it can be read as the simple saga of some vinyl recordings, and the machinery by which those recordings were sent into the air. Yet, maybe in telling the simple story, the more complex one will be revealed. There's an intricately patterned fable beyond the mere tubes, transistors, and troubadours of the sixties and early seventies. There's the tale of a time when virtually everyone of a certain age was tuned in to the message that they were the most important segment of the most powerful country on earth. As these young people grew, their musical language grew in depth and significance, darkness, and impact. The kids who were told they had all the answers also had all the questions. The one big question soon was, Why should we listen to the people who've made a mess of things—our parents, the government, the money-grubbing corporations that support wars, death, and despair? And so they stopped listening. They stopped listening to AM radio too. But before they did, they created a monument—one that will always live in the music of the heyday of Top Forty radio.

The voice of the era when the boom babies were blooming will forever echo on the 45's and the albums that were played for the first time by me and hundreds like me who bombarded the babies with the religion of rock. Let this then be the record of what it was like to be one of those preachers and to serve the industry that understood that the good times had arrived and it was up to us to let them roll.

CHAPTER ONE

Radio Recollections

Radio was always my calling. Like looking at one of those blue-and-red-dot patterns that form a picture when viewed through a piece of red cellophane, I can hold three or four events under my memory's lens and get the picture that radio held a fascination for me far beyond anything else in my youth, far beyond what it held for anyone else I knew. The recollections may not differ from those of any other kid born in 1935, but I believe their vividness does. For me, the beacon of radio in my early life is as bright as it was then. I can see it still.

Come with me to the 1940s:

An air-raid siren is sounding. It's an ominous sound, but one I'm used to. It happens often and, like most seven-year-olds, I've been quick to assimilate these strange new experiences into the norm of my life. This wartime thing isn't exactly normal, but I'm sure I'll survive—as long as the "Japs" I see bayoneting babies on the Movietone news at the Mayfair theater stay out of Brooklyn.

Still, when the sirens sound and my dad covers the radio with a towel, it's as if the war enters the house. The light, dimmed by the worn terry cloth now kept next to the radio for the frequent drills, is an eerie one. Gabriel Heatter seems to be even more distant than usual, maybe unaware that he's talking to us from under a towel. I'm uncomfortable with this new ritual, but I'm certain I mustn't ask that the towel be removed. My grandfather is one of the neighborhood air-raid wardens and I must be a brave soldier in the local version of the conflict, yet I want my friend the radio to be untouched by what seems to be touching everyone. I'm usually as brave as I'm supposed to be, boasting to my younger brother, Bobby, of my greater understanding of global affairs and civil defense, but one day, when I'm alone in the living room, the war reaches out from the radio and grabs me fiercely, shockingly.

It's the afternoon of February 9, 1942. I'm sitting in front of the Philco because I've learned from watching my parents that you can hear the radio only if you look at it. I'm listening to Uncle Don. Uncle Don is my radio cartoon show. Cross-legged, gape-mouthed, I'm in my own world, populated by Uncle Don, his cast of characters, and me. Suddenly a stranger enters. A news announcer has taken Uncle Don's place.

> *"We interrupt this program to bring you the following news bulletin. The* Normandie, *the former French ocean liner recently purchased by the United States government and renamed the* Lafayette, *is burning in New York Harbor. Arson and enemy activity are being investigated. I repeat. The ocean liner* Normandie, *now named the* Lafayette, *is burning in New York Harbor. Arson is suspected."*

The Japs have sunk the Normandie. *What's worse, they've taken Uncle Don off the radio. This is the real thing!*
"Mom!"

Radio brought me the war. From December 7, 1941, until VJ Day, 1945, I learned, in the intuitive way that children learn, the power of radio. Through it, Edward R. Murrow could describe to me the sky over London after a blitz. The great Walter Winchell could put me in the company of "all the ships at sea." And, while listening to Fred Allen or Jack Benny, my family and I could be sure that we'd hear whatever bulletins we needed to know, just as we'd heard of Pearl Harbor. Why, every week on the radio, FDR would chat with me about the fortunes of the Allied forces. The radio brought me close to Mr. President himself, until, finally, it brought me the message of just how close to him I and everyone I knew had been.

I'm walking home from an after-school punchball game on April 12, 1945. I see all the ladies from the neighborhood gathered on Mrs. Bloom's porch. Mrs. Flink is there, Mrs. Goldberg, and my mother too. How odd for them to be out of their houses this near to dinnertime.

As I approach, I hear something I've never heard before—the sound of the radio in the street. Mrs. Bloom has placed her RCA in the front window. Finally close enough to see sadness on the faces of the women, I hear what the newsman is saying.

> *"We interrupt this program to bring you a special news bulletin from CBS World News. . . . President Roosevelt is dead. The president died of a cerebral hemorrhage. All we know so far is that the president died at Warm Springs in Georgia."*

The women weep. I know I'm watching the world change—seeing it on the radio.

Radio brought me this death, and through it an awareness that radio stood for reality. Boston Blackie, Superman, the Bickersons, yes, even The Shadow, these were real people to me. What happened to them mattered, because someday when I grew up I was going to enter the larger world radio represented—the world beyond Brooklyn—and I was going to use what I'd learned on the radio.

COUSIN BRUCIE!

It's 1951 and I'm sixteen years old. For two years I've been attending the Dramatic Workshop, located next to Mamma Leone's restaurant on West Forty-eighth Street in Manhattan. After my magnificent portrayal of Tooth Decay in a school hygiene play, I knew I had a future as a thespian and so begged my parents to allow me to venture to Manhattan to learn my craft. Not long ago, Mrs. Freilicher, my English teacher, recognized the performer in me. Because of her help, I'm able to earn my English credits in the city-sponsored All City Radio Workshop. And so, I spend ten hours a week in dramatic educational productions presented on WNYE-FM in New York. In one performance, I'm the quintessential Paul Bunyan, beefed up on all the delicious training I'm getting and benefiting, even in a radio production, from my puberty-attained full height of six feet, two inches. I'm learning that acting is the key to radio—even if you are merely giving the audience the best performance of yourself.

Radio brought me direction. It ribboned its way through my life until finally it had a grip on me that no persuasion or diversion could loose. At sixteen, I was ready to make a commitment.

I'm at my friend Paula Waksmon's house. I'm telling her mom that I'm going to be a radio personality and I think I'll need a different name—something powerful, something more universal than Meyero-witz, something like "Wayne" or "Cooper" probably. She takes the phone book and opens to the M's because I should at least keep the same initials. Her finger moves down the page. Morrow. That's it. Bruce Morrow.

I'm going to go home to Twenty-ninth Street and tell my parents I want to change my name legally from Bruce Meyerowitz to Bruce Morrow. The trip home to my block is when I realize what risks I'm willing to take for a radio career.

Radio seduced me. Before I was out of my parents' house, it tempted me to believe in myself, to think of myself as capable of being like the idols I listened to—the people regarded as gods in the households of my neighborhood.

Radio and the neighborhood. Monumental forces in my life. In the Brooklyn of my youth, those forces combined to produce legends. Who knows what it was about Brooklyn of the forties and fifties that produced so many notorious characters? My theory is that it was such a tight world, so absolutely circumscribed by traditions brought from other cultures and by coda enacted to keep the neighborhoods peaceful, that it invited testing. How far could you press against the walls of social order? How much freedom was there room for in the narrow corridor of convention? What could you get away with despite the scrutiny of the yenta sentinels? The testing created energy and the energy acted like fire to a cannon fuse. Knowing that we'd tested our acts in the Brooklyn circus, colorful, critical, and crucially supportive, many neighborhood kids kept testing themselves in other arenas—and succeeding. Like so many human cannonballs, stars were hurled out over America. But no matter how far we went, we took with us the romance of that first Brooklyn big top. We romanticized it even further, I suspect. You have only to share a few recollections with me to see how benevolent a Brooklyn boy's memory can be.

CHAPTER TWO

A Jock Grows in Brooklyn

The neighborhood wasn't really more than five blocks. In the Brooklyn of the forties and fifties, the borders of communities were delineated by the distance to the butcher shop, the bakery, the deli. Back in those days, you didn't travel more than four or five blocks before you came upon a full complement of such purveyors, so your everyday world was one that extended only about as far as you could walk in ten minutes.

The core of the neighborhood was "the block." In my first twenty years of life, my family and I lived on two very similar blocks. The first, East Twenty-sixth Street between Avenue V and Avenue W, had at least a hundred houses squeezed next to each other. They were all made of red brick and the people inside were pretty much as alike as the buildings that housed them. The second, East Twenty-ninth Street, was identical in architecture and inhabitants.

Mrs. Bloom, Mrs. Goldberg, and Mrs. Flink on East Twenty-sixth Street washed their laundry in the same brand of detergent, went through the same rituals of meal preparation, took similar summer vacations in the "mountains," and complained about one or another in-law. My mother was one of these women, prettier, I think, and younger than my father by fifteen years, a distinction that made her even more powerful than the traditional Jewish wife. She had been selected for her beauty and spirit as well as her level-headedness, not merely as a sensible partner with whom to share the rigors of getting ahead in the world—the common goal of every family on the block. Abe Meyerowitz was already on his way to having gotten ahead before he married Mina Platzman and she was an able manager of the household she kept for him. Her household soon included two kids who were terrors, one of whom she had to chain to the porch to keep in tow. For a period of time, she'd get calls from one or another lady a couple of blocks away that young Bobby had been spotted running down the street naked. It wasn't that he wasn't properly supervised, it was just that the kid was an escape artist. Not one to be thought poorly of by the neighbors, Mina Meyerowitz put her baby boy on a long lead of the miles of gauze bandage kept in our house to ease the symptoms of my father's phlebitis. My younger brother wasn't exactly *chained* to the porch, but I liked to think of him that way. In our sibling rivalry I took the tack of being above reproach—at least when "they" were looking. I later came to understand the need to test the bounds of Mina and Abe's control. That's no doubt what my younger brother had already caught on to when he took up his wanderings and it's also the plausible explanation for the way we became possessed when they were out of the house.

"Bobby, go get the hose from the backyard. Make sure it's screwed on to the water thing, but don't turn it on yet."

"Why, what are you going to do?"

"We're gonna help Daddy. Go get the hose."

Bobby dispatched to do the harder part of the job, I fetched the laundry detergent from the basement. Earlier that week, my parents had been talking about having the piano tuned and cleaned and I was going to handle the cleaning part of the job.

First, a generous pour of detergent into the top. Now, a command to my brother to turn on the hose attached to the faucet on the outside of the house. Here's where a doomed mission became a disaster beyond imagination. I'd planned on just a small amount of water for me to brush around the inside of the upright. Instead, we had a foaming waterfall cascading out of the piano, onto the floor, spreading across Mom's beloved carpeting.

"Stop. Turn it off. Turn it off, you idiot!"

"What?"

He couldn't hear me over the sound of the faucet. I ran outside. "Turn it off, damn it!" Using the epithet I'd noted as an adult manner of registering rage, I got hapless Bobby's attention and raced back inside. Sure death was soon to follow. There'd be no way to fix this up, though we tried to bail the instrument out with the galvanized buckets from the basement and the soup pots from the kitchen. Mina and Abe came home to a chorus of pleas and prostrations.

"Bruce did it. Bruce told me he was going to help Daddy."

"Shut up. I was cleaning the piano. Bobby didn't turn the water off like he was supposed to."

"He didn't tell me to turn off the water. He only told me to turn it on. I was outside. I didn't see what he was doing."

Bowing, scraping, betraying each other, we pleaded for mercy. I don't remember the punishment, but I'm sure it wasn't merciful.

Such was life inside our house. A life I remember most in terms of Mina, because the house was her realm. Abie Meyerowitz had the M and W Hat Company—designers and manufacturers of "the finest snowsuit hats in America"—as his domain, and, like all the men in the neighborhood, kept a low profile, surfacing as a powerful figure when we ventured into the outside world, a veritable Captain Kirk on our journeys to the uncharted regions of upstate New York or, once every eon or so, to Lakewood, New Jersey. Still, my mother made it clear that Abie's well-being was the primary objective in everything we did. He was the key to all security and the keeper of the keys to his sons' futures.

My grandmother promoted her son-in-law's prominence too: "Go to the bakery and get your father two, no seeds. We've got nice seeded rye, but your father, he always liked rolls. You come straight home like a good boy, Brucie, we'll make the kreplach. It doesn't hurt for a man to know how to make his own kreplach. It won't kill you to know how to make chicken soup either."

I'd negotiate with her before I went on this errand. There was no question that I'd obey, but, once again, there in that tight neighborhood a boy had a need to test, to see how far the rules could be stretched, to see what control he could take for himself: "Mamma, can I have twenty cents if I go?"

"Absolutely not. None of that before dinner."

Ancient human radar at work, she'd know what I wanted the money for. A slice of heaven, Brooklyn's work of chocolate art—seven-layer cake. Promising to wait until after dinner before even taking the tiniest bite, citing merit points from the months of meat loaf and matzo ball K.P., smiling my most winning grandson-of-a-saint smile, one time out of every half-dozen I'd get the two precious dimes. On the way home I'd wrestle with the scent of that cake and fiddle with the tissue wrapping until there was enough icing stuck to it to yield a lick's worth of ecstasy, still true to my promise of no bites. I've had pockets bursting with dimes since those days; I've walked on European streets where the bakeries offered confections that looked like opera sets. Still, none has ever tempted more, or rewarded me greater than the seven-layer cakes won in bargaining sessions over going for "two, no seeds" for my father.

Life outside the house was one of contests as well. The boys of Brooklyn, like boys everywhere, had sports as their proving ground. The gutters were our on-site playgrounds. Only fruits, nerds, old ladies, and babies went to the city playgrounds. What did we need them for? We had the sewer covers to mark out expertise in punchball or stickball. And when we tired of those games, we played king or stoopball. I always knew I'd be able to spot a spy who came into the neighborhood (and I was obsessed with flushing out spies). I wouldn't ask him who played third base for the Dodgers or the Yanks—I'd ask him for the rules of stoopball or what a three-seven shot was. If he was a Brooklyn kid, he'd know. If not, I had him cold.

In the late forties, Brooklyn, yet to attract the developers' attention, also had a number of stunning nature preserves. They were the surface of the moon, Death Valley, the Argonne Forest. They were the "lots"—acres and acres of yet-to-be-developed real estate that represented the war zones between territories.

My gang was the Invincible East Twenty-sixth Street Kids (not exactly a snappy gang name, but to the point and sort of Musketeerish) with a few ringers from East Twenty-seventh because the kids on that block were tougher and we needed them to help us fight. Of course, no girls were allowed, or even considered. This was men's turf and we had men's business to do.

Our moms would pack lunch in brown bags. We may not have had precisely the same food, but our lunches were variations on a theme, the theme being sliced bread and cheap filling. For me, it was usually cream cheese and jelly on white bread. It's a wonder that the prevailing Brooklyn nutritional wisdom didn't kill me. "I've got nice sliced white bread for you, Bruce—eat the crusts too. Just a minute, let me add some more salt to the soup. Tonight we're having steak—good healthy red meat." Out of this kitchen came my sandwich wrapped in Cut-Rite waxed paper and a mayo jar of milk or water and off I'd go to join my comrades, who were similarly fortified.

One particularly difficult battle was the one we'd fight at least once a summer for possession of the East Twenty-ninth Street lot. We had the most sophisticated weaponry known—dirt bombs. The best kind too. Ours were solid enough to travel far and fast, but soft enough to pulverize on impact, thereby temporarily blinding our enemies. We were gentlemen at war.

Never ever did we pack stones inside our dirt bombs, but we heard that the rough kids from East Twenty-fourth Street did. We were never going to fight those guys. The East Twenty-ninth Street crowd was rough enough. Eli Blinderman and Norm Katz were usually hurt in the fistfight that inevitably followed the bombing and, though I was a strong, solid kid, I had lost my taste for hand-to-hand combat on the day when Tommy Shor had blackened my eye for no good reason. Win or lose, I knew my mom would tell me I was "going to get it" when my dad came home from the factory. Summer day after summer day, I'd risk my father's wrath, playing out the war the radio was bringing to me, trying to stretch the bounds of the territory that held me close by the ladies like my mother and grandmother, doing manly things in the company of the other boys who were testing too. Now it seems that every act was a kind of trying the ground mined with the mores of second-generation Jewish Brooklyn, escapades like stopping at Rose Kurtzburg's back window on the way home.

"What do you see, Eli?" (GIGGLE)

"White stuff." (BREATHLESS LAUGHTER)

"Come on, what do you see?" (NEARLY TEARFUL HYSTERIA)

"White stuff like dough in the bakery, and moles on her back and Mrs. Kurtzburg hooking her up. Are you too chicken to look for yourself?

Mrs. Kurtzburg was the girdle-and-brassiere lady who corseted all the neighborhood women. What we saw at her window was usually a woman tugging at folds of flesh and the constraints of woven elastic, heaving heavy breasts, trying to get comfortable in the armor of the undergarment.

What was so hysterical about all of this? There was the titillation of knowing that brassieres and girdles were the front line of the sexual battles we imagined our fathers fighting nightly. It had to be a battle, didn't it? Whatever it was they did, the women subtly suggested they didn't do it willingly. Much more silly than that thought was the performance of a lady you knew only fully clothed, like Mrs. Flink, the lady who regularly admonished us to include her son Jerome (two years and several rituals younger than we) in our play, bumping and grinding her way into something that looked doll-size compared to her bulging bloomered backside.

Weary from the lot wars, we salacious soldiers of misfortune would hang on to Rose Kurtzburg's windowsill by our black-rimmed fingernails until the tickling danger of being discovered combined with the display inside to topple us into her yard in a fit of howling. That would bring her screaming to the window and send us sprinting for the safety of our front porches, where we'd compose ourselves to meet the wrath of our mothers, who hated the dirt we brought with us far more than they loved the sons who'd spent the day collecting it.

These were the weekday diversions. Saturdays had a pattern all their own, a pattern that depended upon whether you could spend a dime or a quarter. For ten cents you could see a movie, for twenty-five, you could spend an entire Saturday afternoon at the Mayfair or the Avenue U theater and see a triple feature, a short about Tahiti, the Movietone news, and coming attractions.

We'd watch Fred Astaire or John Wayne or Esther Williams and eat Good and Plenty candies. I loved the pink ones and saved the whities to be used as missiles to launch at the matron, a sourpuss who was always glowering at the end of the aisle, shouting in a whisper, "Take your feet off the seat. Sit up straight! Stop talking!"

"OK, ready . . . launch! That one almost got her!"

"You boys, you stop that, or I'm going to have the manager down here to eject you from the theater."

Manager of the theater. That had a ring to it. When I got my first movie projector, a toy with a red, blue, and yellow filter that rotated in front of the lens, allowing for color cartoons, I went into the Saturday show business. Barbara, a slightly older Twenty-sixth Street girl, would let me set up chairs in her garage. The kids would pay a nickel and take their seats. I'd sell candy at an outrageous markup, threatening no show if the receipts weren't good enough. My skimpy library of Popeye cartoons shown week after week weren't what brought the kids back for more. It was Barbara's live act that followed our animated feature. She would take her little boy dog and put it lying on its side on a table. Then she'd lift its hind leg and with great seriousness and flare do to the dog what no one would dare tell their mothers we'd seen Barbara do.

Eventually, I was able to leave the immediate village and hunt the distant, verdant territories with the other braves. We traveled by BMT Brighton Line to the most exciting world I've ever known—Coney Island. If I had a dollar fifty, I could get a blue ticket to attach to my belt. This was my passport to all the rides in Steeplechase Park. The horse race, the Giant Slide, or the roller coaster, second in terror only to its neighbor, the world-famous Cyclone, the most perilous roller coaster on earth. *Perilous*, that was the word for so much of what went on at Coney Island. There were the death-defying rides and slides, there was the ever-present mortal danger of spoiling your appetite by washing down your Nathan's hot dogs with three or four bags of their patented crinkly French fries. There were the girls. Yes, girls went to Coney Island too, whole groups of them right there, without the eyes of the neighborhood to watch the sway of their hips, or to note the invitation in their glances. There were even costumed clowns to act as merry matchmakers, prodding the wide-skirted temptresses onto the electric grate over a huge fan that would blow their dresses high around their waists, revealing their legs clear up to the edge of their underpants. Oh, what peril of growing up right on the spot.

Coney Island, practically a caricature to most of America, was a metaphor for life for a Brooklyn boy. There were the tests of courage and strength and skill: the rides and sledge-hammered gongs and toy steam shovels pivoting over seas of shining prizes, waiting for the sureness of your touch on the controls to retrieve the one you wanted most desperately.

There were the first hesitant advances toward the society of the opposite sex, punching your buddies on the arm as you looked at the prettiest girl, wondering how the hell you were going to cut her away from her herd of friends so you could maybe propose the trip through the fun house as a preliminary to one night getting her into the tunnel of love.

Brooklyn gave me the tension that produced the energy of my on-air style. Despite my parents' edict and the neighborhood enforcement of staying with "my own kind," I was just a subway ride away from the relief of riding the skies with all kinds. Fed by the standard leathery gray flank steak or pulpy corned beef of the Flatbush kitchens, I could flee to a deli for knishes or maybe a tongue sandwich and the nectar of a chocolate egg cream. Testing, always testing the impenetrable structure of the second-generation society, I could develop the courage to face down the reasoning that one did something a certain way because "that's how it's done."

I could get one thing more. In the Flatbush of the first years of the fifties, it was possible to get a high school education offered by people who were concerned and focused enough to notice the sort of shy kid who liked to write plays and organize performances. The relentless scrutiny of the block was tempered into watchful observation in the neighborhood school, an observation that pushed me from being an occasionally enterprising kid into a confident director of my fellow students. Somewhere along the line between grammar school and high school graduation, I was given the right arena to marshal my energy into a leadership characteristic. It was right there in Brooklyn I would learn that people would listen to me, they'd believe it would be fun to do what I said would be fun to do.

CHAPTER THREE

The Education of Brucie Morrow

My dad and I had a springtime ritual that probably lasted for a half-dozen of my preteen and teenage years. We'd walk on the boardwalk at Brighton Beach until we got to our favorite sunbathing concession. There we'd pay a quarter each to lie on canvas beach chairs and have the attendants bundle us tightly in blankets. Stretched out, holding reflectors under our chins, we'd drift in and out of conversation, half-dozing in the barely warm sunlight. We'd talk about where we were going to go fishing that summer or about the stock market or the price of a haircut.

Somewhere between the washing of the piano and these days in spring, I'd passed out of the world of the women into the world of the men. I was now fit company for my father, a man who didn't question many things, but who had the quiet sureness of someone whose life had turned out just as he'd supposed it would. His hard work had been rewarded by enough money to keep his family comfortable. We were not to take that comfort for granted. My father's shouldering of responsibility created a responsibility in his sons. It was clear that I was to repay him for his efforts on my behalf with efforts on my own behalf. I was supposed to "make something of myself."

As near as I can pinpoint it, I began to make something of myself when I became Gooba the Caveman.

During my junior year at James Madison High School, I took to heart the challenge of the school sing. A contest among the classes, the sing was to determine the most talented class in the school. There would be skits and talent acts, some students would tap-dance, some would mimic the styles of Sinatra or Crosby. I was at the Dramatic Workshop by this time, being trained in the rudiments of the stage and getting my footing in front of the footlights. As a member of the All City Radio Workshop, I was performing daily for that flyspeck audience with FM receivers. Practically a paid professional, I volunteered to perform on the junior-class team. It was to be my first performance in front of a live audience since grammar school. I dressed as a caveman, arms and legs dangling from a one-shoulder creation, and mimed "Goodnight, Irene." There must have been something about the way I mugged that appealed to my fellow students, my teachers, and the assorted parents present. Gooba was clearly a favorite with the crowd. The applause was nice. The junior-class victory was sweet. The change was nearly instantaneous.

I began carrying my books the way the cool guys carried them, held high with the arm at a right angle to the body, not hanging from a limp arm or clutched tight to the side. The word "leader" cropped up on my report card. I began saying things like, "OK everybody, we're going to Dubrow's after school, and don't forget, this is pickle day." I went back to Camp Swago that summer before my senior year and developed an alter ego known as Chief Sagamore. A young counselor, I'd attend the Friday night campfires in a blanket and headdress, making an entrance from the woods, telling mystical Navajo legends of my own making. It isn't hard to hold nine-year-olds rapt when they're sitting outside around a huge fire with inky sky and diamond summer stars above, but still I began to believe I had a gift for keeping people's attention. I started to think maybe people wanted to hear what I had to say.

This was the young man who would reflect on nothing in particular while holding the sun reflector at precisely the same angle as his father held his, two bound men in Brighton Beach chaise lounges, one of them twice bound. It wasn't only blankets my father was bundled in, but the conventions of Flatbush culture and that tightest of all constraints, the consuming preoccupation with financial security that the Great Depression had etched in young adults of the thirties. His son, on the other hand, acknowledged no bounds. Like the other children of my generation, I'd tested enough to know the old ways weren't necessarily the ways I needed to live by. I'd hung on Rose Kurtzburg's window and lived to tell the tale. I'd challenged the matron for dominance over the Mayfair theater. The sons and daughters of the old world were the torchbearers of a new one. A war had come between my parents' generation and mine. And, just as the fifties would later come to symbolize a giddy embracing of streamlined modernism, the youth of the fifties were giddy about being modern in every way. I may have had a mile-wide conservative streak, but I had a headstrong commitment to knowing and being what was modern.

My unconventional leanings were counterbalanced by my father's conventional wisdom.

"This is the land of opportunity, Bruce. You can be anything you want in America—even president. But first you have to get a good education."

Opportunity and *president* were two words I heard often.

My parents assumed my good education would be gotten in good old Brooklyn—at Brooklyn College. That was fine with me. After all, Brooklyn had been good to me so far. My friends were fun. Coney Island was fun. There were the movie theaters and the gourmet eateries. There was the familiarity. There was the feeling that I was being recognized as somebody who "had something." All this *and* access to Oz. It was right there on the other side of the bridge—magnificent, magical, mystical Manhattan.

I'd been "going into the city" all my life. I assumed I'd work there someday, maybe even make enough money to live there at some point, but for the time being, I was content with the status quo. The family had moved up in life—from East Twenty-sixth to East Twenty-ninth and things were comfortable.

Abe bought me a car when I graduated from high school. What a beauty—a 1948 Ford Tudor, green body with a white hardtop, a Fordamatic with the most important accessory of all, a powerful AM radio. I was now fully equipped to ride smoothly into my future.

In September I rolled gracefully into the role of college man, but I wasn't destined to be graceful or a Brooklyn College man for long. From the moment I got to BC, I knew it wasn't for me. These people were serious. They wanted to teach me things— like French. After about four months of intensive scholarly pursuits that never took me near my French class, I found the classroom. Unfortunately it was the day of the final exam. With my recently acquired conviction that confidence was 90 percent of the battle, I strode into the room, head held high. My good friend Jerry Moss (who went on to become the *M* of A&M Records) waved to me, looking shocked. He was obviously surprised to notice that I too was taking this particular course. I sat down and looked at the exam paper. I signed my name and wrote off the Brooklyn College experience as a mistake.

I'd failed French and I'd also failed to recognize that Brooklyn College had expected more from me than I'd delivered. I flunked out. I was supremely uncomfortable with the feeling of having blown it. I was the organizer, the kid the high school teachers looked to as a monitor. Chief Sagamore, the sage from many mountains west, had screwed up.

Hindsight tells me I learned something from that failure. I learned to make sure I knew what was important to me. Could it be that maybe this downfall was a signal that I had been involved in something that wasn't, in my estimation, truly important? What was important? Radio. Being heard on the radio as I had been at the All City Radio Workshop.

Across the river was a school called New York University. At New York University they had a program called Communication Arts. Gooba goes to Gotham.

New York University circa 1953 was perfect for me. It had a state-of-the-art mentality when it came to the fledgling art of broadcasting, and it had an open-door, hands-on policy, allowing students access to the equipment in their workshops. Those workshops were the key to my success at NYU. I loved technology. I wanted to know how every electrical device worked. I wanted, more than anything, to know everything about radio and television. Here I was able to mess with equipment, to talk to people who loved broadcasting as much as I did. Besides, being on the island of Manhattan, I was where it was all happening. Just forty or so blocks from where I attended classes (I really did attend—I'd learned my lesson) the three radio and television networks were deciding the fate of the communications industry. CBS-Hytron and RCA, meanwhile, were battling for FCC approval of something absolutely amazing—color television. Was it possible? Surely something as wonderful as TV in color could never come right into our homes.

I heard that CBS was having a press conference to demonstrate their system at Leiderkranz Hall. I had to become one of the press immediately. I went to NBC at Rockefeller Center and talked to somebody in the news department. They obviously had overlooked how badly they needed a stringer on the NYU campus, I explained. Fortunately I had radio experience from the renowned All City Radio Workshop and just enough open time in my schedule to take on this vital role for them. When could I have my press credentials?

Press card in hand, I took a notebook along as a prop and sauntered into Leiderkranz Hall trying to look like a blasé member of the Fourth Estate rather than the overeager broadcast-crazed kid I was. Once the demonstration started, all determination to be cool went out the window. They showed a Randolph Scott movie and the color was every bit as vivid as it was at the Avenue U movie theater. More spectacular, though, because it was so unlike anything I'd ever seen before, was a commercial for Campbell's tomato soup. The soup was red! All of this was only preamble to the presentation of *live* color TV. Models in a nearby studio paraded on the television screen. We could actually see that some had blond hair, some were redheads. They carried rainbows of flowers, all of which were garden-perfect in their hues. This wasn't film they were showing, this was live television, something I thought could only happen in black-and-white. I had walked into the future. I left the demonstration convinced that someday people would actually see television programs in color—right in their own living rooms.

How are you going to keep Brucie down on the campus after he's seen color TV? I was really at my wit's end now. There I was, going to college in the city that was making media miracles, and all they would let me do was "play radio." Sitting in class and pretending I was broadcasting wasn't enough for me. I had radio experience, after all. I had changed my name because I was going to be a radio star. I was ready to be on the air.

Fortunately, the Communication Arts program was run by a man who believed in my kind of impatience. He was Professor Robert Emerson and, together with Professor Irving Falk, he recognized in me a determination that seemed worth fostering.

On the day when I cornered him and demanded to know why NYU didn't have a radio station (my dad was paying good money for my education, after all—eighteen dollars a credit!), he said, "Bruce, NYU runs on a budget, and there's no money in the budget for a radio station. God knows, I've tried to get some, but maybe you can do better than I have. Talk to some of the deans. Go see the administrators. Tell them why NYU needs a radio station, how much it will cost, and how you're going to build one."

How much would it cost and how would I build one? Good questions. Questions to which I had the answers because I also had the most necessary ingredient for the birth of a radio station—a magician. His name was Werner Freitag and he was central casting's idea of a mad German scientist. He wore a white lab coat, and spoke with a slightly fiendish Dr. Franken-stein accent. He was a technician at NYU and lived in a world of wires and tubes and lights and bells and buzzers and never seemed to leave his laboratory. He was patient with the gangly freshman who wanted to know everything about anything that could move a voice from point *A* to point *B*. In the case of the radio station I was hoping for, point *A* was the Communication Arts Group Studio on the eighth floor of the East Building and point *B* was the Green Room, the student lounge four floors below.

"So, Werner," I asked before starting out on my fund-raising program, "how could I broadcast into the Green Room?"

"Vell, young man, you vould need vire. Electrical vire, you understand? The kind that you plug the toaster into the vall vith."

"Wire. And what else?"

"Microphone. Speakers. These ve have."

"How much money would I need to buy enough wire?"

"Twenty-five dollars, maybe."

With twenty-five bucks' worth of wire and Werner, I would be in business.

You'd think I was asking for enough money to build a spaceship. Deans, professors, administrators—they all turned me down. Then one day I got my big break—a tremendous rainstorm.

Those were the days when there was still grass and trees and dirt on the NYU campus—the days when a walk from one building to another on a rainy day took a young lad through rivulets and mud puddles. On this one particularly rainy day I had an appointment with a dean who turned out to be fastidious and (what luck!) had a brand-new carpet in his office. I was wearing galoshes. They weren't tidy boots or modern tote-type things; they were gigantic galumphing galoshes—the kind worn by students who still lived at home with mothers who knew their children's deaths would come from eating seasoned food or getting wet feet.

Oblivious to the mess I was tracking with me, I trudged into that dean's office, shook his hand, and gave him my pitch. He listened politely as I dripped mud all over. By the time I realized his discomfort over what my presence was doing to his carpet, it was too late—the damage was done. I probably started my trademark of talking at lightning speed at that very moment. I sped up my request and sloshed out of there, convinced I'd failed again. A couple of weeks later I received a note saying that, based on the dean's recommendation, I'd gotten an allocation to start the first NYU radio station. Either he was impressed with my single-minded devotion to my dream, or he was afraid I'd drip my way into his office again sometime!

Werner sent me to the hardware store for several hundred feet of everyday household AC electrical cord. I then made a deal with the guy who ran the Green Room to let me attach my electrical cable to the back of the old Stromberg-Carlson radio in the lounge. The wire ran up the side of the building and into the "studio," where we had an antique Dynavox turntable, some speakers, and a classic Shure microphone. That's all it took. WCAG—Communication Arts Group—was on the air.

For a couple of hours a day we'd play classical music and make campus and community announcements: "Erroll Garner will be appearing at the Blue Note all this week. And don't forget, tonight our own NYU meets Fordham in a battle for the bragging rights to New York City basketball dominance. The game's at eight P.M. and the gym is going to be packed, so get there early."

We had to be very quiet in the studio while the records were playing because the mike had to be open and placed in front of the speakers. This was pretty primitive, but after about six months, the university newspaper wrote a story about the radio station that could be heard only in the Green Room of the East Building.

There's nothing more motivating in human nature than the desire to have something simply because someone else has it and you can't get it. Suddenly WCAG was in demand. Students and professors came by to hear it. Soon they wanted to know why they couldn't have it broadcast into their dorms and lounges. Our budget was increased to allow us to have better equipment and to run wires to other buildings. Eventually we even hit the big time—we were wired into the main cafeteria!

For all I know, Werner Freitag and I created the first cable network. That's really what it was—yards and yards of electrical cable, over which a bunch of kids "broadcast" music, talk, and sports shows. Within a year we were on the air twelve hours a day—a dozen hours that needed programming. Luckily, we had an extensive classical-music library, obtained the way only a callow youth could—by being too stupid to be afraid to ask.

London Records was the Stradivarius of the classical-recording industry. Nearly every home that had a record player had *Swan Lake* on London Records. Mine did, so I knew that London was the place to call for a collection of classical music that would make WCAG truly sophisticated. I explained that I'd like to feature their recordings on the radio station serving the greater New York University community. I probably neglected to say we were what was called a "carrier current" station, which meant our signal was carried on the weak radio waves present in ordinary household electrical current, rather than broadcast over radio waves. Carrier current stations can be heard only on radios that are near the wires of the system. WCAG was to radio what two cans connected by string are to telephones. Nevertheless, I gave London Records the impression that we were a fifty-thousand-watt powerhouse broadcasting from the highest building on campus, and was invited to their offices, where I was given access to their complete catalog of Full Frequency Range Recordings. FFRRs were the compact discs of their day and still hold their own for sound integrity. It was like inviting a kid who was used to tricycles to pick out a few Rolls-Royces.

There were literally hundreds of albums—mine for the taking—too many to take in one trip, so for days and days I took the subway to London Records (no way you'd risk bruising your Ford Tudor by venturing into the mayhem of midtown) and selected classical music for WCAG. How did I make my choices? Very scientifically. I picked the ones with pretty album covers.

With twelve hours of programming to fill we needed more than Tchaikovsky and a campus calendar, so we branched out into radio journalism. We did public-affairs programs, where we interviewed the university muckety-mucks on the hot school issues. Why was the track-team budget cut? Why can't students smoke in the classrooms? It wasn't *60 Minutes*, but it was our version of controversy, and as confrontational as any student dared be in those days. We also broadcast speeches that were given on campus. We had no trouble setting up our mikes when someone from the university was speaking, but occasionally Professor Emerson or Professor Falk would ask us not to cover a speech given by a guest lecturer. These were the days of the "red peril," and, after all, Greenwich Village was a veritable hotbed of pinko subversive activities. We had to be careful or the commies would take over the station. I learned early on to cooperate with station management, in this case the school administration, if I wanted the pleasure of being on the air.

Fortunately, there was hope for a boy who wanted to be more than a deep voice announcing silky-throated songsters. Fortunately, everything that amounted to anything significant in popular music and radio was in flux. Fortunately, the years I was at NYU were the years when the earth rocked on its radio axis.

In 1953, my freshman year, the national radio playlists included the Ames Brothers, Teresa Brewer, Perry Como, and Doris Day. In 1955, Bill Haley and His Comets soared onto the scene with "Rock Around the Clock." Though Nelson Riddle had a big hit called "Lisbon Antiqua" in 1956, the same year Dean Martin hit with "Memories Are Made of This," Kay Starr signaled something with her recording of "Rock and Roll Waltz" that year. Rock 'n' roll was making itself known and, try as the establishment might to keep the waltz alive, the moon/june/croon era of radio was coming to a close.

Yes, by 1957 a group called the Crickets had a hit called "That'll Be the Day." Elvis Presley was a fixture on the charts and the brothers Everly were sounding the alarm with "Wake Up, Little Susie." Buddy Holly, Elvis, Don, and Phil were southern boys, sons of the source of race music. These musicians understood the true roots of rock 'n' roll—rhythm and blues. Rhythm and blues was a tragically underexposed national treasure, because it came from the people who definitely were not in the musical mainstream—the "colored" people, as they were called in those days. Geniuses like Big Joe Turner, LaVern Baker, and the Crows were playing to dark audiences and maybe a couple of dozen progressive white devotees, performing extraordinary music that was recorded on obscure labels, if at all. The American recording scene of the fifties was not about black man's music, but the emerging recording geniuses were. Rockabilly was just a page out of gospel and in Cleveland, of all places, a man who billed himself as Moondog had brought the R&B greats to the lily-white ears of WJW's audience by playing tunes released on independent labels. He drew tens of thousands of kids to halls that couldn't hold them with unheard-of integrated bills featuring music that just cried out to be heard.

By 1957, when Moondog was using his given name of Alan Freed on WINS, New York, and I was ready to test my own ability to have an impact on the industry I loved, the times weren't changin', they'd changed. Mr. Freed had shown New York and America that a radio personality could help create the personality of radio. I wanted to be a part of this new kind of radio. I would pledge my life to whatever real radio station would have me just to broadcast the music that was so absolutely compelling. I wanted to be a rock jock and the first place to give me a chance was as ironic a choice as I could make. I was going to champion the music that owed almost everything to black people in a place where blacks were considered inferior to whites. Bruce Morrow was on his way to Bermuda.

Chapter Four

Trouble in Paradise

Did I have what it took to make it in professional radio? Did I have the determination to get hired, become a paid announcer, and, eventually, advance to one of those few big-city jobs—the only positions that had any meaning to me?

In June 1957 I was asking these questions of myself and the world was asking them of me. I wasn't Bruce the wonder kid anymore. I was just another kid looking for a break.

I had my demo tapes. I had my track record of getting what I wanted. I had my dream. I had my share of don't-call-us-we'll-call-you conversations. Elvis might have made his way onto the charts, but, with the exception of Alan Freed, it was still people like Martin Block who were announcing those charts. I'd grown up with the venerable Mr. Block, host of WNEW's *Make Believe Ballroom*. On Saturdays Martin Block would pronounce the week's hit parade in his basso profundo voice, at best indifferent to the music he was touting, at times noticeably disdainful. No one had caught on yet that the juxtaposition of the Voice-of-God delivery with the joyful sounds of rock wasn't long for this world. I wasn't long for this world either, if Dad's hard-earned tuition money didn't yield a job.

I sent out six more demo tapes, this time to stations beyond the borders of the Big Apple. These tapes were about ten minutes long and I thought they were real masterpieces, spotlighting my ability to deliver commercials, introduce records, read the news, and engage in sidesplitting chatter. Six replies came back rapidly. Three said sorry, no positions available, and three said they were interested. One station was in Texas, one was in Panama City, Florida, and the third was in Bermuda.

I knew Texas wasn't for me. I'd never said "Yup" in my life and I was pretty sure I hated horses that didn't pull carriages through Central Park. As for Panama City, Florida, my side of the phone conversation with the owner and general manager of that particular station went something like this:

"Yes sir, I am willing to start on the ground floor. . . . Next week? Of course. . . . Sure, I expected to be at the station eight hours a day. . . . Four hours at *what* car wash?"

It seemed he also owned a car wash and neophyte jocks were expected to polish bumpers as well as spin records. I passed on that opportunity.

Besides, neither Texas nor Florida seemed very worldly and I'd recently decided that at age twenty-one it was time to leave the confinement of East Twenty-ninth Street for the experience to be garnered in the outside world. This made Bermuda especially appealing. Wasn't that the place where the sand was pink and the sky was always blue? Didn't they have lots of girls in bathing suits down there? It sounded like a full-time Doris Day movie to me.

I called ZBM radio, Hamilton, Bermuda, and said I was very interested. Ken Belton, the station comptroller, explained that even on that British island they viewed New York radio as a pipeline from Mecca, and that the tape I'd sent him sounded like the authentic big-city sound that was sorely absent from his station. Ken said that while Bermuda wasn't exactly progressive, the station management was aware that radio was changing rapidly. They knew contemporary music by people like Bill Haley and the Everly Brothers signaled the beginning of a new era and they thought a young announcer from New York could help put them in touch with what was happening. Bermudians were not provincial people, he added. Their island was a haven for very sophisticated travelers. The people of Bermuda were also travelers themselves. Many of them made frequent trips to England and the States. They'd been exposed to life beyond their insular twenty-one-square-mile borders.

He also said he'd set everything up for my arrival two weeks later. Lodging would also be arranged.

In two weeks I would be in Bermuda. If this didn't sound real to me, it sounded impossible to Mom and Dad. Who knew what those people ate? How did I expect to have clean underwear without Mina to do my laundry? Those island people didn't wear shoes. A boy would surely get athlete's foot (or something worse—hoof-in-mouth disease probably). As far as they were concerned, I was going into uncharted territory.

To my mind, concern was the wrong response to uncharted territory—anticipation was what was called for. I anticipated being the Moondog of the Atlantic, bringing the rock word to the unschooled. I also anticipated the joy of going a step beyond the philosophy of Flatbush. I was going to transcend the barriers of Brooklyn by actually springing over them. I would probably need an ocean to separate me from the neighborhood influence. Never mind that I'd probably only actually ventured out of New York State a dozen times and that my idea of a beach was Coney Island or Brighton Beach; I was going to fit right in on those pink sandy shores populated by eager nubile nymphets in scant-skirted swimsuits. There were other barriers I wanted to scale besides those presented by the geography of my youth and the nearly insurmountable odds against one day landing a plum radio slot. At age twenty-one I was ready to have the bevy of beauties that *Playboy* magazine was promising me. In 1956, a French guy named Vadim had made a movie called *And God Created Women*. It was about an eighteen-year-old girl who couldn't get enough of men, an eighteen-year-old portrayed by a pout-lipped blonde named Bardot. The film's action took place on the beach in St. Tropez. The film's reaction took place in movie houses all over the world and in the groins of every red-blooded American boy I knew. To put it bluntly, I was hot to trot, and a tropical isle away from the mores of the many Minas of my neighborhood seemed like the perfect racetrack for the young stud I fancied myself to be.

By the time the Lockheed Constellation touched down on the runway to my destiny, my heart was pounding a signal that my confidence was waning just a bit. What was I doing?

I stepped out onto the shimmering tarmac and knew I might as well have traveled to a new planet. Nothing looked or felt like anything I'd experienced before. The sky was vast, with no skyscrapers to contain it. The light was brighter than any I remembered seeing anywhere else. We're not in New York anymore, Toto. British-accented customs agents shuffled me and my luggage through oh-so-formal formalities and pointed the way to the tiniest taxi I'd ever seen. The ride to ZBM, however, began to ease my mind. Everything was so pretty. The houses were little pastel palaces. The trees and bushes and flowers looked like they'd been brought for a movie set. Most of all, it looked so clean. The Brooklyn housewives would approve.

I was surprised when the driver told me we'd arrived at the station. All I saw were the tiny buildings of downtown Hamilton. Apparently I was headed for the second floor of a small office building. I walked up a narrow flight of stairs and into a modest reception room. I asked for Mr. Belton and sensed immediately from the way the petite receptionist gaped at me that I was not going to be exactly inconspicuous in this world of diminutive, veddy proper English types.

"Welcome, Bruce, welcome." The voice came bursting

through the door before the man did. Ken Belton was every bit as ebullient and kind as he was enthusiastic. We'd start with a station tour, he said, then get me settled. The tour of the station was as brief as the quarters were tiny. There were two air studios and one large production studio. The equipment wasn't exactly state of the art, but it was more professional than what I'd used at NYU. Although I was disappointed that my first job was turning out to be in munchkin land instead of in one of the steel skyscrapers I'd aspired to, I felt as though I would be comfortable in this place that was rather homey, and like everything else on Bermuda, sparkling from recent whitewashing.

"Now we need to find you a place to live," Ken announced after the tour.

"What do you mean 'find'? I thought this was all arranged." Dad was right. These were savages. I'd wind up sleeping in the streets.

We walked about three blocks from the station to Mrs. Larsen's boardinghouse. Ken had once resided there and he thought the "nice" old lady would put me up too.

Mrs. Larsen was a round, rosy-complexioned woman with a thick brogue. She sized me up and said, "Twenty-seven dollars and fifty cents a week. You can use one inch of tub water a day. I'll show you your room." Was I right in thinking my closet in Brooklyn had been bigger? Probably I was just tired from the flight. Ken left me to unpack and I folded myself over to lie on the bed under the slant in the roof. A knock at the door.

"Excuse me—I have your linens."

Ah, the maid. No, Mrs. Larsen's daughter. Her name was Rhonda and she was lovely. This was a figure that was meant to be seen in a swimsuit. I even detected a resemblance to Bardot. Everything was going to be all right after all.

But I had a few things to learn about Bermuda.

The first hint came one afternoon on Mrs. Larsen's porch. I'd been there only a short while, but long enough for my landlady to learn my love for shepherd's pie. She also made me generous breakfasts, and it was in the middle of one of these feasts when her conversation turned to keeping Bermuda "pure."

"We don't want Jews on the island," she said.

I can't remember hearing very many phrases that were more sickening to me in my life. My head swam from the vertigo that overcomes one when a revelation is almost too dreadful to be fully taken in. My friend, my surrogate mom, was a bigot. I asked her to repeat what she'd said and she did.

I'd never been confronted with one-on-one anti-Semitism before and I was momentarily flooded with confusion. Should I keep my mouth shut and dismiss this as the stupidity and narrow-mindedness of a provincial old woman? No, I had to say something. After all, I'd seen Gregory Peck in *Gentleman's Agreement*. I had to do what he'd do.

"Mrs. Larsen, do you really like me?" I asked.

"Of course, dear, very much."

"Mrs. Larsen, I'm Jewish."

She started laughing. "You are not—you're just playing a bit of a joke, you rascal. I know what Jewish people look like. I know what they act like too."

But one look at my expression of hurt and anger and she knew I was dead serious.

After that morning I got the barest of breakfasts and the special shepherd's pies ceased. Mrs. Larsen and I exchanged only brief words. There was enough hypocritical graciousness bred into the Bermuda innkeeper to keep her civil to me, but not enough open-mindedness to allow her to recognize that she'd liked me before she found out my background. While I continued to live in that boardinghouse, too proud, too stubborn, and yes, too lazy to seek out something that might feel more hospitable, its doors were symbolically closed to me. I was an outsider of the worst sort—one who's been marked as an undesirable—and perhaps that set the tone for my whole experience on Bermuda.

While the ZBM experience was not without its light moments, like my announcing of the "football" (soccer) scores and the slapstick comedy that inevitably followed when nearly every station employee from the mailboy to the program manager would burst through the studio doors yelling things like, "That's *Birming*-ahm, not Bir-ming-*ham*, you dolt!" Or the Sunday morning when I left the feed from the turntable open while the *Let's Go to Church Show* was being piped in from a nearby chapel. Instead of monitoring the worship service, I was auditioning sound effects for dramatic war stories I was to produce the next week. In the midst of the gospel, I was inadvertently broadcasting sirens, bombs, and screams, sending the island's elderly and shut-ins into a frenzy of terrified phone calling to the police and fire departments.

Lucky for me, station management was tolerant of a new kid, and even more lucky, Ken Belton was watching over me.

After a short while at ZBM, it had become clear to Ken that my niche was in playing avant-garde rock music and that my forte was my ability to create calm out of the chaos of live broadcasting.

"You seem able to do more than spin discs, my friend," he said one day. "What kind of live program would you propose for yourself, old man?"

It didn't take me long to dream up a format. I knew live dance shows were catching on in the States and I wanted to give that a try. We called our show *Search Party* and invited listeners to come to the studio to dance to the music of local performers and the latest rock releases.

It was a hugely successful show, owing in no small part to how little there was for teens to do in Bermuda. However, in providing something for the young people of Bermuda to do, we'd provided something for the bigots of Bermuda to fester about. After a few weeks of *Search Party*, I began to get phone calls and letters subtly suggesting it might be unsuitable to have black youngsters at events where there were white youngsters, lest "mixed dancing" take place.

To the station's everlasting credit, they let the show—and the mixed dancing—go on. The protests escalated.

First, I heard from a high school principal.

"You are an Ike worshiper!"

"A what?"

"Ike . . . Ike . . . your president, you nigger lover!"

I felt that vertigo again. It wasn't a few backward old ladies who were prejudiced on this island.

Within days there was another call.

"Watch yourself, cheesehead [another endearing term that Bermudians had for Americans]. Be careful how you walk home tonight."

Talk about the wrong thing to say to a young Yankee who was weaned on John Wayne and Jimmy Cagney, and a veteran of the Lot Wars to boot. I armed myself with a lead pipe and literally didn't go anywhere without it. Walking home at night I retaliated against many a shadow of swaying palm, giving out with a battle cry that was part karate, part Comanche, and mostly fright.

The physical assault never came, but the battering of my spirit continued. Just a few years after getting my confidence from playing cavemen and Navajo sages, I was getting the stuffing knocked out of me by real life. Bruce Morrow, child of the thirties and forties, young adult of the fifties who'd never had to take a political stand in his life, was facing political issues on a daily basis now. In the house I'd grown up in, sticking with your own kind was another way of saying we didn't really have to think about the "coloreds" or the under-privileged—they were outside of the gates and we had enough to tend to on the inside—but being an outsider on Bermuda I was forced to face the plight of other outsiders and, inevitably, I was forced to take a stand.

One day a church with an all-black congregation burned down. The pastor came to see me and explained that he had heard that I was sympathetic to his people. Could I think of a way to help him rebuild his church?

I knew if I put the right amount of effort into helping that pastor, I'd be off the island in a matter of weeks (by force or by government invitation). I knew if I didn't help rebuild the church I would be choosing to stand on a side of the color line that was not only morally reprehensible, but would mean that for the rest of my career I'd have to live with being a hypocrite.

Having had that upbringing bounded by things as simple as never going outside of the streets numbered twenty-four or thirty or beyond those lettered *U* or *Y*, I never had to know much about civil rights. I never even thought about black people as people with homes, families, churches. But I did think about and know about race records and nonwhite entertainers, and I did understand that the fires of change that were blazing through the music industry had started with a spark struck by nonwhites. Without R&B there was no rock 'n' roll. Without blacks there was no R&B.

I know I didn't sit and reason my decision through on the basis of what Big Joe Turner would think, but when I reflect on it now, it seems to me that rock music was an instrument of my awareness that the country I grew up in had some citizens who not only weren't "my kind," they weren't my color either. They had status, though. They had importance because they were making themselves heard. Against all odds, against the prevailing wisdom of the small world of Brooklyn, Bermuda, and virtually every place in between and beyond, these people were influencing one of the most influential of all forces—popular music.

I told the minister I'd throw the biggest record hop Bermuda had ever seen and we'd charge admission and try to get donations of refreshments, for which we could also charge. I would try to get the station's support, I promised, hoping that my guardian angel, Mr. Belton, would stay angelic for just one more devilish bit of Morrow madness.

"This is my swan song, Ken. I wasn't meant to stay around much longer, so how about letting me go out with a bang?"

"You sure can get yourself into trouble, old man, but I guess I asked for trouble when I went looking for somebody like Mr. Freed. Go to it!"

Carte Blanche! Or, in this case, Carte Noire!

We found an empty warehouse in Hamilton and the station lent a ton of air time to promoting the Rockin-est Record Hop Ever:

"The latest American releases, live entertainment, dance contests, prizes, and a rocking good time. Don't miss it!"

Thousands came, paid, danced, and enjoyed themselves. We raised nearly ten thousand dollars—which went a long way toward rebuilding a simple chapel on a complex island.

Within two weeks, Mrs. Larsen had her slant-ceilinged room back, ZBM had an opening for a more sedate air personality, and Bermuda had its status quo.

I had started the process of being grown-up Bruce Morrow and I had learned what my homeland meant to me. Not bad for about twelve months and, all in all, when I look back on it, not a bad twelve months at that.

CHAPTER FIVE

Winning and Losing on WINS

After the Battle of Bermuda, I prepared a résumé that painted me as a jock of all trades. I stressed my management and producer roles at NYU. I boasted about all the sales experience I'd bring to any station fortunate enough to get my nod. (Well, I *did* have sales experience. It was I who'd convinced Sal the Eighth Street Barber that advertising on WCAG would bring the New York University men flocking to his establishment.) I painted myself as the wizard of the wireless, the man who'd brought rock radio to Bermuda's world-renowned powerhouse station. Testing the strands of credibility, Bruce Morrow on paper became as amazing as anyone who'd ever been on the air.

WINS was looking for a producer. They wanted somebody young and eager (and cheap). I was all that, and I was one thing more. I was a WINS freak. This was the era when WINS was the number-one station in New York. They'd gotten to the top by understanding two things about radio.

The first thing was a concept called Top Forty. Top Forty was to rock radio what talkies were to film—the thing that gave it life.

The story that is told in the radio business is that Todd Storz, owner of the Storz radio chain in the Midwest, was in a bar with one of his station managers, Bill Stewart. After a while, Storz and Stewart noticed that the bar patrons were playing the same songs over and over again on the jukebox. They counted and found that only about forty songs were ever played more than once a night. Those forty were played repeatedly, however, and about ten of them were played again and again and again. If these customers (who looked like the type of listeners Storz stations were trying to attract) liked to hear forty records over and over again in a bar, that just might be a good radio format. There also might be something in the concept of the Top Ten. That's how Top Forty radio came to be—out of a bar in Nebraska!

WINS had observed the success of the Storz stations in the Midwest and had imported a guy named Mel Leeds from their Kansas City operation. By hiring Mel Leeds as program director, the WINS management demonstrated an insight into the future of radio and a willingness to do what every great rock station was to do for the next decade—learn and adapt from other stations' successes.

Understanding the revolutionary potential of Top Forty was integral to the dominance of WINS radio, but the most significant thing WINS understood was the importance of one man. His name was Alan Freed.

When he died, broke and broken down at the age of forty-three, Alan Freed took his truth with him. What was left to the living was legend, exaggeration, and the kind of fiction that becomes fact after someone dies. Alan Freed made many friends and as many enemies in the broadcast business. His friends would tell us that he invented rock 'n' roll, literally coining the phrase and trying to copyright it. His enemies would speak of his arrest during the payola scandal of 1960 and the underhanded dealings that event confirmed. The truth about the man probably lies somewhere in between Alan Freed's image as the immaculate conceiver of a musical revolution and his indictment as the murderer of rock radio as it existed in the fifties.

He was unquestionably a man who understood music and knew the difference between saccharin and sophistication. It seems as though his early training as a trombonist and his appreciation of the big-band sounds led him to look for danceable music to play on his show on WJW, the most important radio station in Cleveland in 1951. Either intuition or the advice of a record-store owner led Freed to the music that wasn't being heard on radio—the "race" music being played by those dark-skinned artists whom young Buddy Holly was discovering. Alan Freed was definitely a risk taker and it seems sure that he understood the importance of rhythm and blues. He also understood it to be his responsibility to get it played on the radio. As Cleveland's "Moondog"—not exactly a safe, buttoned-down Caucasian stage name—Alan Freed became one of the bravest men ever to be a part of the radio industry. There can be no question that it was a kind of integrity that led him to play the R&B music that no one else would touch. There was an honesty about him in those early days that wouldn't let him fudge what he was offering his audience as the best of the latest music. He knew the major labels were rereleasing beige, bland versions of songs that were so much more powerful when rendered by their "negro" creators. Because of his stubborn focus on what was real in music, Alan Freed forced the folks waltzing down the middle of America's recording road to march to the different drum of black people's music. He forced them by pounding on telephone books as he did his show, pounding out the tribal beat he knew could not be ignored. He was a showman with a cowbell, talking straight at the audience and defying indifference. He hawked his wares and preached the praises of his freaks, the musicians no one had ever heard of before, all the while using the show as a medium for the message about the beauty of R&B, not as a platform for himself. There were safer ways to be a radio personality in the fifties. Alan Freed took the dangerous route—the one that led him to be the crusader for the creators of rock rather than the peddler of white artists who covered their songs.

Pounding on his telephone book, he eventually pounded his way into the consciousness of the nationwide radio industry and WINS New York. In 1954, WINS brought Freed to New York and handed him a much bigger phone book and a much bigger audience. His *Rock 'n' Roll Party* was one of my school-rooms. I studied the way his jive patter was deceptively low-key. There was unmistakable energy there, a kind of nervousness that was belied by the cool-cat lingo. I couldn't put my finger on it, but what I intuitively sensed was that Alan Freed was being more *himself* than anyone I'd ever noticed on the air before. His was not announcing from a safe distance like the formidable Martin Block at WNEW, nor was he cozy like Peter Tripp, "the curly-headed kid in the third row." No, Alan Freed was anxiously sincere, and sincerely anxious. His jive patter rang true, as if he were a high school kid using slang in an overwhelming desire to be accepted as someone in the know. Mr. Moondog communicated a shorthand message of earnestness that got through to urban young people. I also loved his obvious power over everything that happened on his show, almost as if he weren't working for a radio station, but more that he was giving them the privilege of presenting him. I loved the predictable unpredictability of it all. There was no way to know exactly what would happen on a Freed show and no way not to know that something good was bound to happen. It was from Alan Freed that I learned there could be a kind of controlled frenzy—something I felt inside myself, but hadn't yet named or developed.

For over four years, Alan Freed was the 7 to 11 P.M. force behind the success of WINS, and though he'd gone to WABC by the time WINS gave me the nod in 1958, it was Alan Freed's aura that suffused that offer for me. It didn't matter that I wasn't going to be on the air. I was overwhelmed to be going to the home of Jack Lacy and Stan Z. Burns. I was going to be a producer for the station that had brought Moondog to New York—Ten Ten WINS!

Thank goodness for blind enthusiasm, because a semieducated ape could have handled my producer duties and the equipment at WINS. The radio industry has grown so rapidly and has become the forefront of so much technology that the stations of just twenty-five years ago are more like centuries removed from the modern operations of the eighties. The equipment I worked with doesn't even show up in the most outdated, backwoods daytimer stations. Most notable among what would now be beyond anachronisms were the ETs, which were so outlandish that the latter-day Spielberg creation probably *could* have phoned home on them.

In those days, commercials and public-service announcements came to radio stations on ten- or fifteen-inch discs called electrical transcriptions. These metal or plastic plates were usually played from the inside out, just the opposite from the way a 45 or LP is played, on machines that were about as streamlined as my grandmother's wringer washing machine. The playing arm was a sort of metal club, the "stylus" more like a claw. A revolving pizza tray spun the disc. When it was time to play a commercial or public-service announcement, the engineer would hit a switch on the turntable and spin the right disc. How did he get the right disc? That's where young, eager, educated, experienced Bruce Morrow came in.

My job was to look at the log, the schedule that a radio show runs by, and pull out all the discs that were necessary for a show. I'd put them in order and stack them next to the engineer so when the air personality turned the show over for an announcement, they'd be ready. Not exactly an Einsteinian challenge, but I *was* working at a New York station and, as it turned out, I was at the right place at the right time.

About six months after I got to WINS, AFTRA, the American Federation of Television and Radio Artists, went on strike. All the announcers and newspeople walked out of all of the radio stations in the city. Management went on the air—a bunch of business types spinning records and doing news. Without a tape of those actual broadcasts, I can conjure up a mythical sales manager or higher-up trying to keep a show rolling. Everyone has seen and heard what happens when microphones are handed over to the uninitiated:

"Uh, let's see . . . I guess it's time to tell you the weather. Uh, let's see, it's seventy-one degrees and cloudy and it says here we might have showers later on. Yes, that's what it says. Seventy-one degrees. Cloudy and, er . . . um . . . showers predicted for later on. OK . . . that was the weather . . . now it's time to play a record. Let's see. Here's 'Little Star' by the Elegants. I guess we'll play that. Here's 'Little Star' by the Elegants."

Dead air would have been better. Certainly the kid who had gone to the All City Radio Workshop, the former star of WCAG at New York University, the famous air personality in Bermuda, *was* better.

I got a great shift, 2 to 8 P.M. and I milked it. I did news. I talked music. I was a performer onstage in New York—the big time—and I wanted to be loved!

I had something else going for me. I had nothing to lose. I didn't know how long the strike would last, but for as long as it did, I was going to be the best I'd ever been—the best stand-in that ever was. I was going to test myself in a trial by fire—with the most important shift on the most important rock station in the city.

In retrospect, only youth would have allowed me to take that test, since it took a kind of innocence to have the unthinking reaction that a strike was my lucky break. Where it might seem that it took supreme confidence to go on the air, it was actually a lack of confidence that carried me across the picket lines. It was only because I did not yet feel like a member of the fraternity of New York radio performers that I could identify with management and walk into the station every day. My walk across those picket lines followed me for a long time after I'd "made it" in the business. Colleagues wondered how nice a guy I could really be if I had been willing to be a scab to get on the air. Looking back, I both see how it must have looked and feel what I probably felt. In the memories of some, there must be a picture of the tall, arrogant kid striding past the air staff to take his place in front of the microphone. My perception was that I hadn't yet earned my place among the picketers and, as a kid hired as part of management, I had the responsibility to do what management did. Management went on the air during a strike.

If, as a nearly three-decade member of AFTRA, I'm now not entirely comfortable with having been on the air during that time, I was as snug as Cinderella in her glass slipper while it was happening, and as fearless as hell. I didn't mind taking on one of the most beloved characters in the history of New York City—Fiorello La Guardia. Who hasn't seen the newsreels of Mayor La Guardia reading the comics on the radio when the newspapers went out on strike during his administration? While AFTRA was on strike, the Newspaper Guild went out again, taking the comics with them. If I could give the people their funnies, I reasoned, I could make them love me the way they'd loved the Little Flower.

I went down to the *Journal American* and gave a guy ten dollars to sneak me out a galley of the first comics that would be released when the strike was over. In these lawyer-infested times, I'd probably be sued for some breach of copyright or infringement of something or other, but I had a former mayor as my inspiration, and the belief that I was doing a public service as my protection. Booty in hand, I sat in the studio reading "Puck the Comic Weekly" as if I were reciting Shakespeare, complete with different voices for different characters, just the way an old Uncle Don fan would. La Guardia had played it straight; I had to one-up him somehow. I put in some sound effects and I was as corny as the subject matter. I read all the comics that day on WINS. Mel Leeds was in the studio faster than Watson made it to Alexander Graham Bell. This felt like trouble. Leeds was smiling, however, and delighted to report that for the first time since the strike had started the phone calls to the station weren't suggesting that any settlement was worth it to get the management bozos off the air. True to the excessive personality of a program director whose ass is getting saved, he wanted me to do the comics again right away. Not different comics, however; the station wasn't about to spring for a ten-buck bribe or about to risk endorsing a return trip to the *Journal American* building. So, I read the same comics, did some more shtick and hammed it up all over again. The phones rang in approval that was music to my ears.

In Bermuda I had been a fish out of water, my beached wails reaching too many people who didn't want to hear that the future was on the way. In New York City, I was obviously in my natural habitat. That bit of phoned-in audience approval told me that if I was allowed to do what I'd been preparing to do—give the best possible performance of myself—I'd be a star. I felt loved, and as with the beginning of any love affair, the beloved becomes better than the mere mortal.

Energized enough to give Con Edison a boost, my normally rapid speech pattern became a runaway train. Giddy with success, excitement, the thrill of it all, I developed an involuntary vocal reaction; that is, occasionally I simply had to screech. "Yeeeeeeeeee!" I'd bellow. It felt like a giant Coney Island of a career was beginning for me. The kind of noise one gives out on an amusement-park ride was entirely appropriate to the situation. Little by little the teenagers began to notice that, for the first time, the guy on the radio sounded like one of them— a kid with energy to burn with a voice as frantic as the passage of puberty felt. I was having my initiation into adulthood before their very ears, and they hooked on to my sound and to me, calling the studios with requests, telling the operators they liked that crazy guy Morrow. July 1958. "Sweet Little Sixteen" by Chuck Berry. "All I Have to Do Is Dream" by the Everly Brothers. "Twilight Time" by the Platters. Dream come true by a guy named Bruce and some kids who could identify with him.

Five or six weeks into the strike, Mel Leeds called me into his office. He said, "You're no longer a producer here. You're fired."

Flunking out of Brooklyn College couldn't hold a candle to the feeling that overcame me when Leeds uttered those words. Screwing up was one thing; rejection was a whole other matter. How had I failed? I was fired. How many times have how many millions of people wanted to reply to that news, "You're joking"? True to the luck that surrounded my experiences at WINS to date, Mel Leeds was.

"The strike is about to end," he said. "You're through as a producer because I'm putting you on staff as an announcer. You will now be making eighteen thousand dollars a year."

Eighteen thousand dollars a year! It was Michael Anthony giving a new millionaire the news from John Beresford Tipton! For one of the few times in my life, I was speechless. I asked Mel to call my father.

"My dad's my agent," I declared.

So Abe, the hat manufacturer from Brooklyn, came up to the station. He wore his best suit. He didn't talk much, but he listened hard. He asked if I'd have a contract. (Not yet.) And if I'd have to join a union. Nobody in our family had ever belonged to a union. (Not yet, either.) Then he shook hands with Mel Leeds. Then I shook hands with Mel Leeds. Then I shook my dad's hand. Then I hugged him. We were a long way from paying a quarter for a beach chair and a reflector.

The neighborhood changed for me once I was a bona fide radio personality. Mina let the word out in her subtle way, telling the Humann Meat Market that she was in the market for some nice steak for her son's dinner when he came home from being on the radio, probably promising a "plug" in return for special cuts and fast delivery. We never waited in line at the deli again. Sam, the head waiter, assigned himself to our table on a permanent basis—no novice lox slingers for the new radio star. It was heady stuff at first, but after a few months of getting used to my new celebrity status, I began to feel comfortable in my career. Up until this time I'd pretty much flown by the seat of my pants, but now I was getting a sense of being a trained radio pilot.

First of all, there was the time of my shift—7 to 11 P.M., Freed's former slot. When people ask if I'm a morning person or night person, I honestly have to answer I'm both. I'm a morning person for my own life and a night person for other people's. During the daylight hours I keep to myself, puttering with my photography or video equipment, wandering around the city, taking it all in alone. At night I love relating to other people. Never having had a normal job, I never really understood the nine-to-five life of the city, but I could feel what people were doing after seven. I could sit at the mike and see the ladies doing the dishes. I could feel the night shift at work. I knew about the cops taking a break in a diner and the kids in their rooms doing everything but their homework. Guys driving on the Long Island Expressway or, in the summer, heading for the Jersey shore; couples parked and making out—I could feel them, understand them. I could talk right to them because I was with them.

I wanted my audience to be able to see me, to feel me, to know me also. I felt I wanted to give them a picture of me beyond what my voice told them of me. I wanted to have something that was mine and mine alone so I could be picked out from among all the other voices coming out of the magic box. I wanted people to relate to me. *Relate* turned out to be the magic word.

At this time, anyone could wander into a radio studio; the stations thought it was good public relations and since there was a guard in the building and lots of people around (and since it was a simpler, safer time) nothing too bad could happen. One night an elderly black lady looked into the studio window and motioned to me that she wanted to come in. She looked tired but sane and I pointed to the door and motioned to her to come in.

"I'm cold. Can I sit down?" she asked.

Wondering if my initial friendliness was going to turn into a night of visiting with someone who was obviously not a rock 'n' roll fan and probably not here to speak with the hot young rock jock, I answered, "Yes ma'am. You just have to be quiet when that light goes on."

"I won't be stayin' long," she replied.

This was good news. I went about my business, studying the log, preparing to announce the next record.

After I closed the mike and the light went off, she asked, "Do you believe all people are related?"

"Yes, I do. I really do," I said. I really did, despite my stick-with-your-own-kind upbringing and the Mrs. Larsens of the world.

"Well, cousin, can you give me fifty cents please? I want to get home to the Bronx." I gave her two quarters and she left.

I went on with the show, feeling pretty good that I'd helped a sweet old lady, but thinking nothing much of it. That night I drove home to Brooklyn as I had so many times before. The Brooklyn-Battery Tunnel went by barely noted. The noise of the streets and traffic was the same as always, a rushing tinny sound, the running water of a day's end. There was an extra sound, though. I heard it in the distance, in the part of my brain that was already carrying the day's experiences into the memory compartment. Like a wakened sleeper trying to identify the lingering impression of yesterday, I tried to conjure the source of the vague excitement I felt. What was it that had hit a bell in my mind?

Cousin. That woman had called me "cousin." That was it. I had what I had been looking for. My listeners would know me better, would feel that I was different because they were going to be related to me. I was going to be their Cousin Bruce.

The next day I told Mel Leeds about my godsent message. "I'm going to be Cousin Bruce Morrow on the air, Mel."

"You're nuts. You know how corny that is? This is New York City, not Kansas or Cleveland. Play it straight, kid. They'll laugh you off the air if you don't."

"I know New York, Mel. You're the one who worked in Kansas. This city is cornier than anyplace on earth. God knows Brooklyn is corny. People cheer when they hear the name Brooklyn. New Jersey is corny. Real people are corny. There's nothing wrong with that. It's fun. Let me try it for a couple of days."

Experience met enthusiasm and convinced itself that it was best to just let things like this run their course. Mel grumbled and told me to keep it to a minimum.

That night in 1959, I played it to the hilt. "This is your Cousin Bruce and for all you cousins everywhere I have what you want—the music, the magic, and the message. And now . . . right here on Ten Ten WINS, your Cousin Brucie gives you the King. Here's Elvis. . . .

I not only was Cousin Bruce Morrow. I'd become Cousin Brucie. In a matter of days it was clear that I'd be Cousin Brucie for the rest of my career.

Mail came addressed to Cousin Brucie—lots more mail than ever before (not a little of it asking for a loan for a member of the family). When people in stores or restaurants recognized my voice, they'd say, "You're Cousin Brucie. Hi, Cousin!"

Guys at the station started calling me Cousin and salespeople started pitching Cousin Brucie's show. When advertisers asked for Cousin Brucie to do their spots, it was settled forever.

It's likely that a scared young man from far away had the courage to approach WINS only because he'd heard the character who called himself Cousin and thought he could talk with him. He was a sixteen-year-old budding songwriter from Canada who had visited New York and stayed with members of a Canadian-bred band called the Rovers. While in the city, he'd gotten his friends' producer, Don Costa of ABC Paramount Records, interested enough in a song of his to have a test pressing made. He'd also heard the Cousin Brucie show.

A determined young man, he'd gone back to Canada to get his Uncle John to represent him, and one day they appeared in the lobby of the WINS building on Central Park West. They'd come directly from the airport because Uncle John thought they had no time to waste if they were going to speak with the fast-talking radio announcer his nephew was so keen on. The sight of the kid and his uncle and their suitcases probably charmed the guard, because from his description I knew I should let them up.

Once in the studio, the boy was struck with an attack of the shys. Uncle John did all the talking. Young Paul was really talented, he said. Would I just listen to his record?

I listened and it was good. It had that simple calypso beat that was so critical to success in those days. It had a boy-loves-girl story. It had lyrics that could be understood and remembered after just one hearing. It had something different— a Canadian who actually wrote his own material—at age sixteen, yet!

I put it on the air immediately.

"My friends, I have something very, very special for you, a brand-new recording, never before heard anywhere in the world, by a young man you're going to be hearing a lot from. I predict that this song is going straight to the top of the charts, my dear cousins. Tell me what you think. Here's 'Diana' by young Paul Anka."

Listen, even if it went nowhere, a young boy had had his dream come true. His record was being played on New York City's top rock 'n' roll station. But this song was definitely going somewhere. The phones lit up. The listeners loved "Diana." It looked like young Paul Anka might just have a ride on the rock rocket.

Rick Sklar, the WINS assistant program director, was in the studio by this time. He too was won over by Paul and Uncle John, so the song was put on the WINS playlist on the spot.

Contrary to popular belief, magic isn't a complicated thing. No, it's actually easier for magic to happen when the situation is straightforward. The wheels of "Diana" 's success turned very easily. Within hours, kids who'd heard the record on WINS were asking for it in record stores. Other stations in New

York that regularly monitored WINS had heard "Diana" and were greeting Paul, Uncle John, and their test pressing with open arms. Stations in other cities monitored New York station playlists, and in the few short days it took the production recordings to reach them and record stores across America, the song was already soaring to number one.

What would have happened if the shy young kid and his assertive uncle hadn't known about a deejay called Cousin? The same thing probably, but maybe a little slower without the supportiveness that the family thing implied.

I've thought lots of time over the years about the phenomenon of people embracing the persona of Cousin Brucie. The structure of modern families seems to explain it. Having brothers and sisters gives you an early taste of the meaning of love-hate relationships. There's always competition on some level. There's the wanting Mom and Dad's undivided attention, but having to share it with that creep, pest, brat who shares the house with you. There are fights over pieces of cake, drumsticks, and what TV program you're going to watch. But your cousins—now that's a different matter. You see your cousins on holidays when there's lots of excitement and plenty of cookies. Cousins have neat toys that you don't have and their parents make them share. Sometimes you get to sleep over at their house and eat stuff your mother doesn't cook. A cousin is a celebration! It's a family without the feud.

Too bad not everybody at WINS was happy to have a celebration right there at the same station. There was one person who was very unhappy to have a new cousin. In fact he sensed that this wave of familial devotion from the fans might drown him. His name was Murray Kaufman.

Part of the enormous void left by Alan Freed's departure from WINS was that of an authority figure. Freed spoke the lingo and the tempo of the music he played. Freed was a white black man, cool, smooth, unruffled. In 1959, another ambitious guy, this one named Murray, took the late-night slot. This was a smart guy who understood that the association with the savvy of the blacks was a benefit to an air personality. Mr. Kaufman became "Murray the K," as cool a cat as ever mugged in front of a mike. If Freed was a preacher, Murray was a pied piper. He piped out a special language that turned his name into Mee-uh-zuray the Kee-uh-zay, a somewhat African language that gave young listeners a code unbreakable by the parents who were already railing against the noise that was all of a sudden passing for music. Murray understood the passions of youth as well. What better thing to do on a summer night that drips with desire than take in the submarine races? Submarine races were contests that, since they couldn't be seen, were best watched while embracing—preferably in the backseat of a car. Yes, Murray had come up with a delightful euphemism for all degrees of sexual encounter, and teenagers tuned him in to be at the races with them. He was the ultimate troop leader with a language and an understanding to offer. Murray gave kids exactly what they wanted—acknowledgment that they were growing up and license to hold on to some of the secret rituals of childhood.

He was different on the air, the embodiment of the seriocomic sentiment of the early days of rock radio:

> "This is Murray the K on your Swingin' Soiree. The music is ready to take you there. Are you ready to go? Let me hear it then [CUE TAPE-RECORDED AT BROOKLYN FOX THEATER: 'Ahhh-Bay! Unh! Ahhhh-Bay! Unh! Koo Eee Sowa Sowa!'] Here's something for all the submarine-race watchers in Plum Beach, New York, from Kathy Young and the Innocents, 'A Thousand Stars.' "

Meeuhzuray the Keeuhzay, the wizard of the wee hours, was also insecure as hell. He didn't like the noise that was being made about this kid who called himself Cousin. He didn't like knowing his good friend Irving Rosenthal, proprietor of Palisades Park, who had gotten him his job at WINS, was now asking for Cousin Brucie to do appearances at the park.

I appreciated Murray on the air. He was a showman. Off mike he was not a nice man, though, so I maintained a respectful distance. Still, I was apparently getting too close for Mr. Kaufman's comfort. What happened between us was like a scene in a melodrama about conniving corporate types. Murray decided he wanted my shift. Obviously he couldn't convince management that I didn't have a following, but with the help of a certain executive, maybe my popularity with the advertisers could slip a bit. Suddenly my show had fewer commercials than usual.

Murray's cohort was eager to give Hap Anderson, the station manager, an explanation. The advertisers were complaining, he said; my delivery was too fast to make their spots understood. There was a solution, of course. Give Murray Bruce's shift. Murray's delivery was intelligible. He would bring the advertisers back.

A station manager's first responsibility is to keep the money coming in. Hap told Mel Leeds to tell me I was out.

"You're out of seven-to-eleven, Bruce," Leeds said. "Murray's in. We can sell lots more spots if Murray has that slot. Something's happened to your appeal with the sponsors, I guess. You can have eleven-to-three if you want it."

Brilliant move, offering me the graveyard shift. Only by talking bubble gum had Murray the K made something of that slot, but I wasn't Murray. I wanted my people, my cousins, at 7 to 11 or nothing. I got nothing.

Cousin Bruce Morrow was off the air.

How had Murray Kaufman been able to fiddle with the commercial load? Why didn't Mel Leeds stick up for me and say I was doing well?

Do I know for sure that money changed hands between Murray and anyone else? I only know what I observed and experienced during that time and what a grand jury soon found out about the radio and record industry during an investigation in 1960. Soon the media knew about it too. They called it payola.

While I was at WINS, I was certainly aware of the boost Mel Leeds had given my career and I felt encouraged to remember who had promoted me from lowly producer to soaring air personality. Who knows what could happen to a young disc jockey? He could mess up on the air and need the program director to go to bat for him. Some hotshot from Chicago might send in a demo tape that sounded pretty appealing. A kid could get sick or take a vacation and his replacement could get in the good graces of management. Then there were the appearances, commercials, station promos to be doled out—all that additional exposure could mean a lot to a jock. It took a lot of time and work on the part of the program director to handle all these "extras." If you wanted a guy's help, you had to earn it.

When Mrs. Leeds opened an art gallery on Madison Avenue, her dutiful husband wanted to help her succeed. He also wanted some of his young announcers to have the benefit of investing in art. He strongly suggested which paintings would be perfect for our apartments.

That's not too terrible, is it? Lots of people in lots of businesses stay in the good graces of people who can help them by supporting their favorite charities. It's a kind of graymail— an encouragement to contribute. Unfortunately, Mel's favorite charity was often himself. Mel Leeds was probably part villain and part victim. He surely was the victim of a weak character at a time when it was practically impossible for a guy with any power over what got played on a major-market station to avoid being bombarded with cash and "gifts."

As rock grew and the power of rock to make money grew, the power of rock to corrupt grew too. The big record labels had the big artists; those artists were going to get played on the air no matter what. But what of the medium-size and small labels, with struggling, obscure artists? How could they get air play? Unfortunately, things were happening too fast for them to happen logically or well. Literally hundreds of records from hundreds of cities, towns, and post-office boxes around the country arrived at every major radio station in America every day. Dozens of others came in the briefcases of people called record promoters.

Record promoters worked on salary plus bonuses. The more money their label made, the more money they made. The only way for the label to make money was for their records to sell, and the only way the records would sell would be if they were first heard. With stations playing the Top Forty tunes and no more than twenty up-and-coming tunes, the chances of a record making it to the air strictly on merit were as slim as the records themselves. And so the record promoters encouraged various radio-station employees to play their records. The greatest amount of encouragement went to the people with the most power—the program directors. Disc jockeys were naturally the next-most-powerful people at the stations. Before formats got tighter than Tina Turner's skirts (in part a direct result of payola), a jock could pick a song he thought would make it and spotlight it on his show. I saw disc jockeys leave the station with television sets, with cases of liquor, with smiles on their faces that seemed to be inspired by more than a good day at the studio. At Christmastime, limos arrived to take people and their booty home. "Booze, broads, whatever ya want"—this was a standard offer.

How did I escape? Dumb luck. I was too small a fish when payola hit its pinnacle, a kid starting out at WINS. By the time it was over, Murray the K was investigated and copped a plea, Mel Leeds was indicted by a grand jury along with five New York deejays and a music librarian who'd had a lavish wedding. Alan Freed took the fall, and was broken forever after.

Murray had other things going, however. There were his friendships with the people who could keep him where he wanted to be and there was an ability to get around the rules. Anyone who has a copy of the Bobby Darin recording of "Splish Splash" can check and see who got a publishing credit, and therefore a cut of the royalties. I believe it was a man named Kaufman.

In the era of pay for play, when records entered radio stations wrapped in cash, when air personalities "co-produced" records, when Christmas gifts had to be hauled home in trucks, did Murray the K pay for my shift on WINS? It certainly wouldn't have been an alien act considering the times and the people involved.

Whatever had happened, Murray had 7 to 11 on WINS and I had to find a job.

CHAPTER SIX

Palm Reading

Miami Beach, Florida, has an aroma that is as artificial as the sight of towering hotels at the ocean's edge is jarring. Chlorine, air conditioning, floor wax, and Brasso wipe out the salty sea scents one expects on the Florida coastline. For a boy used to the wafting perfume of pastrami and exhaust fumes, it is the scent of a foreign land. Still, I smelled the possibility of finally establishing my career in Miami. After my departure from WINS, I took a job at WINZ, serving south Florida.

THE MAN WHO CAPTURED NEW YORK CITY IS COMING TO MIAMI! HERE COMES YOUR COUSIN BRUCIE! read the newspaper ads.

Cousin Brucie. The man who captured New York City. WINZ evidently believed in me—particularly in their advertising. These guys didn't consider me a kid whose shift could be lifted. I was a man to them, the man who'd captured America's most important radio market.

I was also a married man.

Those first shining moments as a staff jock at WINS had given me an identity as both Cousin Brucie and as the guy for whom the deli waiter saved the leanest corned beef. This was the guy who now took girls out on dates, a guy seemingly with the world on a string, but not without some down-to-earth longings. Like my audience wrapped up in the sweetly simplistic lyrics of the times, I wanted to find my "Venus." I didn't want to be a "Lonely Boy"; I believed in a "Dream Lover."

Susan Stoloff was a Belle Harbor girl. Blond, lovely, voluptuous, Susan was enthusiastic about my career. She believed in a me I was only just getting to know, a fish who was testing himself in bigger ponds. It didn't take long for me to want to be married to the nice girl who shared my dreams of untold radio success. And so we were married. And so, unquestioningly, Susan packed up our barely lived married life and dutifully moved down the eastern profile of the continent with me—to a place that might as well have been in another country.

In 1960 one of the crowning glories of Miami Beach was the Eden Roc Hotel. It was in a suite at the Eden Roc that (courtesy of WINZ) Mr. and Mrs. Morrow were first housed, trying to imagine themselves equal to the protocols and pretenses of life in a Miami Beach monument. For all its opulence (there was enough room to run a couple of radio stations in that suite, and enough fruit from the hotel management to start a corner produce stand), the Eden Roc was no place to begin a marriage. There is nothing more uncomfortable for a couple whose dates were in the small Chinese restaurants on Mott Street or the tiny neighborhood Italian places in Brooklyn than to be thrown into the vast diaphanously decorated dining room of the Eden Roc. Worse than that, nothing could be less private than the swimming pool, with its dozens of chaise lounges set out like an elaborate card game, where, under the watchful eyes of people who made a profession of being hotel guests, Susan and I tried to conduct our hesitant newlywedded conversations. We tried not to look just married, but it was impossible not to in the company of vacationing yentas with radar-equipped nuptial detectors. Once they discovered our status, the pool sharks zeroed in on targets in need of all kinds of advice.

"Radio? What kind of business is that for a nice young man? Get yourself established in an office. Go into manufacturing. Such a pretty young girl . . . she needs security. There's no security in that loud music."

Susan and I quickly contacted real estate agents and just as quickly decided to rent an apartment in a "luxury complex" just off Biscayne Bay in Miami. Squeaky clean, wall-to-walled, spacious, furnished in just-married modern and the booty of a bodacious Brooklyn wedding, our home was to be Susan's career. I was a radio personality who could "provide" for his bride. The conventional wisdom of 1960 indicated that there was no need for her to work. My work wasn't much more stimulating than housework, it turned out.

Though there was a ratings war raging in Miami—"This is Rick Shaw on WQAM—Miami's favorite station!" "This is Big Daddy on WMBM—Miami's FAVORITE station!" "This is your Cousin Brucie on WINZ—Miami's FAVORITE STATION!"— there was no real edge to anything. Here at the continent's edge the people had come to settle down and to settle for what excitement filtered down from the Northeast. Nothing was originating in Miami but the shipments of oranges sent north by tourists.

After a few short months in the Sunshine State, I'd drive to my Saturday night parties—live from the station's studios "high atop the lovely Biscayne Terrace motor hotel"—with the feeling that I could imagine a bank teller brings to his daily job. In the studio I'd talk with the kids and chatter over the record intros, the same talk, the same chatter I'd used in my buoyant Big Apple broadcasts. But without the buoyancy. The kids were teenagers, just as the New York live audiences had been, but they were shyer, less sassy with me—into an almost private dating ritual of a radio dance party, rather than seizing the chance to perform in front of a microphone the way the New York kids had. I was hard put to draw these polite southerners into the spirit of live radio. They looked like Ricky Nelson's audiences on Ozzie and Harriet's weekly show. Where were the screaming meemies from the Ed Sullivan Elvis broadcasts when you needed them? I was a 45 RPM deejay in a 33 1/3 town.

Where was the excitement of being a radio personality? In Jamaica. Not Queens. West Indies.

In the nighttime, WINZ, Miami, bounced off of the ionosphere onto the island of Jamaica. There the locals grooved on the American who talked fast and played the latest tunes from Stateside. A Miami citizen who found himself in Kingston would be shocked to hear the jingles of his hometown radio station and the cacophony of the guy who usually came out of his car radio while he was driving over the MacArthur Causeway. Two Miami citizens were thrilled when this experience happened to them one Kingston night. Their names were Sid and Louis Merenstein, a father-and-son team of promoters who understood the question that typified the decade that was beginning—"why not?"

Why not get the zany WINZ disc jockey down to Jamaica to do live broadcasts? The locals seemed to dig the guy and the music. Why not find the money to be made in this? Why not try to get the sponsorship that could make this a venture that would be beneficial for all concerned? They came up with the *Pepsi-Cola Cousin Brucie Saturday Night Party*, to be broadcast live from The Glass Bucket Club in Kingston, Jamaica, every other weekend. Jamaica. It sounded like a fine adventure to me. Every other Saturday I'd fly to Kingston, spend the afternoon setting up and the evening rocking with the Jamaicans on RJR and JBC, Kingston. I was back doing island radio, but it was different this time. For one thing, Jamaicans were not Bermudians. These people were as free as people get, and in fact, my dance party in Kingston felt more comfortable to me than the one I was doing in Miami. Jamaicans carry their security inside themselves. Where Miamians seemed to be forever tied to living in that balmy, tranquilizing atmosphere, Jamaicans were always talking about going somewhere, seeing something, doing something. They loved to talk about New York. They loved to talk about music too.

It's no wonder. Their island was home to wonderful steel

bands and calypsonians and later gave the world reggae. Within a few years of that first taste of what was to become my lifelong love for Jamaica, a young man named Bob Marley would form the Wailing Rudeboys and later the Wailers. What goes around comes around. Black music had been the seeds of rock 'n' roll. Black men like Marley would later take those seeds and the simple blossoms that were being put forth in the States and turn them into the intricate vines of a whole musical genre that lilted and tilted and had a life all its own.

I was not yet perceptive enough to intellectualize the comfort I felt when I did my shows from Jamaica. All I knew was that it felt good to be among people who had an emotional reaction to the show and the music. It also felt good to be both a radio-station employee and an autonomous performer. I was getting a taste of free-lancing, a taste I'd crave for the rest of my career.

One day in Miami I had an emotional reaction that started the wheels moving in a northerly direction. A Brooklyn boy I'd gotten to know in New York came to town to appear at one of the beach hotels. His name was Neil Sedaka. When he was at Abraham Lincoln High, Neil had put together a group of singers called the Tokens—a group that went on to hit with "Tonight I Fell in Love" and "The Lion Sleeps Tonight." Neil had also gotten a lot of notice in the business as a songwriter. He'd written "Stupid Cupid" and "Fallin'," two tunes recorded by Connie Francis in 1958, but 1959 was really his year. That's when he wrote a song about a rock 'n' roll fanatic. Her name was Carol Klein and the song's title was "Oh! Carol." Carol was a real noodge, the story goes, following groups like the Tokens all over Brooklyn.

"Oh! Carol, I am but a fool. Darlin' you love me, though I treat you cruel." Teenagers all over America knew those lyrics. Carols all over America hoped that the cruel Lotharios of their lives felt, as Neil said, "if you leave me, I will surely die."

The smart young "fool" had his start with that song and Carol Klein didn't do too badly either. She went on to become

Cousin Mommy and Cousin Baby

Getting bitten by the broadcast bug at the All City Radio Workshop

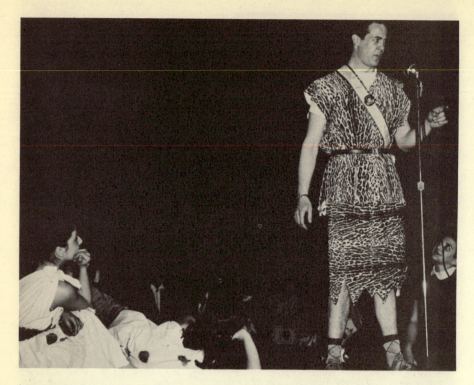

I stopped being shy the moment I became Gooba the Caveman in the class sing at James Madison High.

John Barrymore,
watch out!

My dad taught me how to fish and how to tell fish stories.

BRUCE MORROW

presents

THE WINS OFFICIAL MUSIC SURVEY

NEW YORK'S 40 MOST LISTENED TO TUNES

January 11 1960

1.	Why	Frankie Avalon
2.	El Paso	Marty Robbins
3.	Running Bear	Johnny Preston
4.	The Big Hurt	Toni Fisher
5.	Pretty Blue Eyes	Steve Lawrence
6.	Way Down Yonder In New Orleans	Freddie Cannon
7.	The Village Of St Bernadette	Andy Williams
8.	It's Time To Cry	Paul Anka
9.	Among My Souvenirs	Connie Francis
10.	Bonnie Came Back	Duane Eddy
11.	You Got What It Takes	Merv Johnson
12.	Go Jimmy Go	Jimmy Clanton
13.	Where Or When	Dion & The Belmonts
14.	Not One Minute More	Della Reese
15.	Oh Carol	Neil Sedaka
16.	Smokie (art two)	Bill Blacks' Combo
17.	Shimmy Shimmy KoKo Bop	Little Anthony
18.	First Name Initial	Annette
19.	Sandy	Larry Hall
20.	We Got Love	Bobby Rydell
21.	Heartaches By The Number	Guy Mitchell
22.	I Can't Say Goodbye	The Fireflies
23.	How About That	Dee Clark
24.	Talk That Talk	Jackie Wilson
25.	A Year Ago Tonight	The Crests
26.	Teardrop	Santo & Johnny
27.	This Friendly World	Fabian
28.	What About Us	The Coasters
29.	I Wanna Be Loved	Ricky Nelson
30.	Tracy's Theme	Spencer Ross
31.	Do Re Mi	Mitch Miller/A Bryant
32.	Down By The Station	The Four Preps
33.	What In The Worlds' Come Over You	Jack Scott
34.	Tell Her For Me	Adam Wade
35.	Baciare Baciare	Dorothy Collins
36.	Just Come Home	Hugo & Luigi
37.	If I Had A Girl	Rod Lauren
38.	He'll Have To Go	Jim Reeves
39.	Scarlet Ribbons	The Browns
40.	Misty	Johnny Mathis

PIC HIT: I Know What God Is
           Perry Como

WATCH THIS
Country Boy   Fats Domino
Manana   La Vern Baker

WINS put Bruce Morrow on the air in New York, and on their free music surveys too.

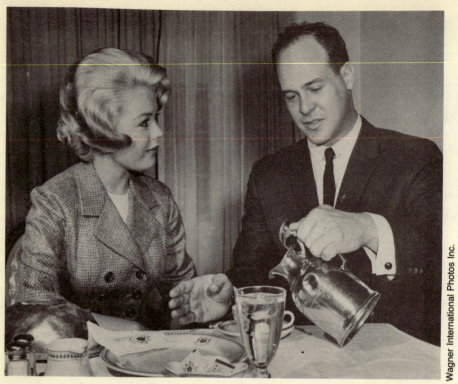

Look at me with Sandra Dee!

Ed Hill

Palisades Park fans loved Muffin Morrow the Wonder Dog, and so did my tailor.

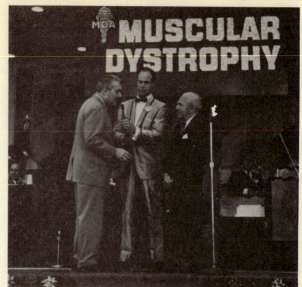

Irving Rosenthal, impresario of Palisades Park (right), got involved in everything from hot-dog sales to the Muscular Dystrophy Telethon.

Saturday dance contests at Palisades Park could literally be a pain in the butt.

Ed Hill

Tony Bennett was as gracious as anyone who ever stepped on that Palisades stage.

...ecutive committee of the Cousin Brucie Fan Club often held their meetings ...sades Park.

Dion and a guy in sensational shoes before a Palisades show

Ed Hill

Ed Hill

The guy with a tear in his eye—Jackie
Wilson

The irrepressible Mr. Rosenthal papered the
city with advertising for the Saturday shows
at his beloved park.

Clint "Rowdy" Eastwood and Paul "Wishbone" Brinegar brought *Rawhide* to Palisades.

Ed Hill

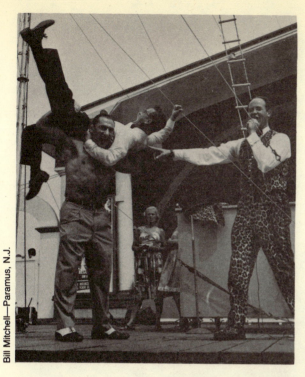

Palisades pal world wres-
tling champion Antonino
Rocca giving Charlie Greer
a lift

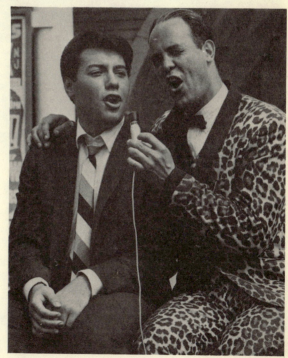

Tony Orlando and tone-deaf
friend warm up for the
show.

Ed Hill

The girls went crazy for Frankie Avalon.

Ed Hill

One of Neil Sedaka's many crowd-pleasing appearances at Palisades

Ed Hill

And I fell in love down at Palisades Park.

Helihopping with WABC's Rick Sklar during the whirlwind Principal of the Year contest

Brucie Lisa illustrated the fans' ingenuity in the Draw the *Mona Lisa* contest on WABC.

Oh, those department-store appearances!

The All-Americans loved safe boating. (Left to right) Herb Oscar Anderson, Scott Muni, Bob Lewis, Miss Safe Boating, Cousin Brucie, Dan Ingram, Sam Holman.

Take us out to the ball game. (Left to right, standing) Charlie Greer, Dan Ingram, Scott Muni, Cousin Brucie. (Left to right, kneeling) Sam Holman, Bob Lewis, Herb Oscar Anderson.

In 1962, everybody hurried to his or her favorite record store for the WABC Silver Dollar Sound Survey.

Carole King and wrote some of rock's classics: "Will You Love Me Tomorrow?," "Take Good Care of My Baby," and "Loco-Motion," among dozens of others. Her *Tapestry* album also became a legend. It was on *Billboard*'s charts for 302 weeks.

Apparently she got over Neil's cruel treatment.

Neil's visit to Miami was like a breath of fresh Flatbush air for me. There we sat, in a studio with a view of the pregnant skyline of America's most dramatic mating of the desire for the serene with the itch to cash in on it, two kids who had emerged from their neighborhoods with the cocky belief that rock 'n' roll was invented to be their stage. We were experts on the topics we expounded on that day—the brilliance of Brenda Lee, the significance of Brian Hyland's "Itsy Bitsy Teenie Weenie Yellow Polkadot Bikini," the indomitableness of Elvis. Rock may have originated in the South, been given life in Cleveland, and continued to be produced everywhere from Philly to Nashville to California, but it was on the streets of New York where it got its legs. The hits were being hurled out of the radio stations of Manhattan and Neil and I knew all about that.

Though we went on to share many public and private stages in our continuing careers, as colleagues, as friends, and as neighbors both in New York City and upstate New York, Neil Sedaka and I were probably never again as close as that evening when we were two young men trying to sound like we had a handle on what was happening to us. We were joined by innocent cockiness that night. Ours was the hopeless confidence that we understood everything that could be known about something that was changing the world as we knew it. Little did we know that the simple beat of rock could be the sustaining heartbeat and life's blood of our careers, or that the naïve rhythm that seemed like such a blissful balloon in music's and history's sky was going to be the very weather of a time, of a generation. We said good-night on the air and wished each other luck. Neil had a show to do at the Fontainebleu and I had to get home to lonesome Susan, so our words after the broadcast were brief and wrapped in the assurance that we'd get together "back in the city." Back in the city. That's what I wanted more than anything I could ever remember.

The longing came to a head with a few months left to run on my yearlong contract. I experienced a mysterious malaise. I became lightheaded. I had unexplainable bouts of anger. It was a case of Hollow Holidays—the phenomenon of Miami at Christmastime. For me, it was like being in the Twilight Zone.

Anyone who has grown up north of the Mason-Dixon line experiences Christmas as a contrast of the colorful with the colorless. December is when the sun is lowest in the northern sky, when the landscape gets the dimmest, grayest light. The trees are bare, except for the evergreens, which are their most austere in that cold illumination. Like wilderness animals, humans take on winter coats that blend with the environment. They wear the gray of the city pavement or the navy blue of the early-arriving night. Minked matrons meld nicely with the leather interiors they inhabit during the winter months.

Into this scene Christmas introduces red, green, tinsel, gold. Oh, welcome colors! Oh, joyous glistening! Just when the bleakness seems about to lock into place forever, a heavenly blessing—a holiday season that sparkles and glows with at least visual (and sometimes downright spiritual) warmth. Never mind that Bethlehem is in the desert. Christmas was made for northern climes.

For a northerner, Christmas in Miami is a contradiction at best, a nausea at worst. Like milk and pizza, or cream soda and sardines, some things cannot be stomached together.

For me, the sight of palm trees hung with Christmas lights, reindeer prancing atop pink bungalows, and Santa ringing his bell on Collins Avenue, just steps off of the sand, was as grating as fingernails on a blackboard. I knew early on that I didn't belong in Miami, but when that first Christmas came, I knew I wouldn't survive another. Oranges in Christmas stockings only worked for me when the stockings were hung near fireplaces that were needed for warmth from the correct Christmas chill.

Once again, the tapes and résumés were prepared, this time to be sent north. This time it was different. I was "seasoned"—literally and figuratively.

I'd been on WINS—the number-one station in the nation's number-one market. I'd been on one of the top stations in Miami, and enough people were finding out about Murray Kaufman's *modus operandi* to suspect that my departure to Florida hadn't been a voluntary gesture to get a year-round tan.

Finally, I received a telegram. It was from Hal Neal, the vice-president and general manager of WABC radio in New York. He was inviting me to join his staff of WABC personalities. The words of that telegram I most vividly remember were COME HOME.

Ask anybody who was alive during World War II what they think of when they hear the word *telegram* and you'll get a reply that translates into "bad news." Our parents, our neighbors, our relatives, all dreaded telegrams: "Please, please God, don't let us hear from the War Department." That was a very real prayer during the war. I'd learned from my folks that telegrams were awful.

The exception to telegram phobia is found among show-business people. For them, telegrams bring good luck, greetings, or messages of congratulations. Those yellow butterflies from Western Union have winged news of bookings at the Palace to vaudevillians and new film offers to actors on location. Remember *Yankee Doodle Dandy* with James Cagney? There's a scene of a play within the movie when the exiled jockey, Little Johnny Jones, waits to see a skyrocket in hopes that he can go back to his beloved Broadway.

Well, that telegram from Hal Neal was my skyrocket. It was then that I knew I was going back to Broadway, Brooklyn, Greenwich Village, and all the city in between. It was that message from Hal Neal that took me out of exile and officially put me in show biz.

Susan and I celebrated at a Chinese restaurant that night. Then, in the midst of this moo goo gai pan parade of an evening, there came a ray of disturbing reality: I had a contract. What if I was unable to wrench myself free to get home to New York? Was I caught in a Miami vise?

We left the restaurant a little worried. I stayed up watching an old movie on TV. "I have to leave town or my wife is going to crack up," the film's hero said. There was my answer.

Well, it was pretty close to true. This was the time of Castro's Cuba. Our apartment complex had filled with wealthy pro-Batista Cubans who were fleeing the revolution. Cuban doctors were working as waiters in Miami. Their wives were adjusting to life in comparatively cramped quarters without a domestic staff of half a dozen. These neighbors didn't have the inclination or the English to socialize with young transplanted New Yorkers. Susan was lonely and left alone on the nights when she didn't feel like coming to the station to help answer the phones. Even more isolating, her husband was in the West Indies every other weekend.

What is a little white lie? If you despise lying, is there any such thing? I suppose if you can convince yourself that an exaggeration of the truth will hurt no one and help someone, that's a white lie. I convinced myself that if I continued at WINZ my work would suffer and the station would suffer. Better also to lose a relatively new disc jockey than one who's become established, right? It wasn't like I was being opportunistic. In 1960, WABC was almost a dog—the eighth or ninth station in the market. They had this new guy named Ingram who everybody said was great, but still, they weren't WINS or WMCA.

I went to the station management with tears in my eyes: "I've got to get out of town or my wife is going to crack up." (Luckily these guys started work at 9 A.M. and didn't catch the *Late Late Show*.) They understood I had no choice. I had to give them two weeks to find a replacement, but they would release me from my contract.

I was free. I was going back home, home to show biz. I was going to what would become the showiest radio station in the history of the radio business. The station that would rock the world, the broadcast cradle of rock 'n' roll, and as much a part of rock history as the music itself. Cousin Brucie was on his way to W-Amazing-B-C!

CHAPTER SEVEN

W-Amazing-B-C

America circa 1961: an energized adolescent waking from a sleep he didn't realize he needed. Eisenhower had marched back to Gettysburg, the anachronism gone back to the beloved battlefield. Taking his place in the White House was a forty-four-year-old telling everybody to stretch. Stretch your sense of responsibility—ask not what your country can do for you. Stretch your bodies—go on fifty-mile hikes. Stretch your world—join something called the Peace Corps and spend a couple of years teaching Rhodesians about irrigation. Shoot for the moon. And expect to land there before the end of the decade.

New York City circa 1961: home to four powerful newspapers: the *Herald Tribune*, the *Daily News*, the *Journal American*, and the gray lady herself—*The New York Times*. Center of three vying television networks (with NBC and CBS head and shoulders above the weakling ABC network) putting out such stimulating fare as *The Many Loves of Dobie Gillis* (co-starring Warren Beatty as Milton Armitage, for you trivia freaks) and

My Three Sons, with Sullivan, Paar, and Lucy still the royalty of the tube. Famed for its New York Yankees and long-departed Brooklyn Dodgers. Run by Robert F. Wagner.

What did the country and the city have in common? A desire to be heard. With the wars and police actions behind us, with the economy in full swing, with a cocky view of America's position in the world and responsibility to the people of the world, we became chatterboxes. No longer the silent, watching youngster in the company of the older, wiser, more mature world powers, America was brazenly talking. New York City, headquarters of American broadcasting, was the logical place for the talking to be raised to the art form that was pop radio. The country had a personality all of a sudden. New York City was dripping with personality. The new era of broadcasting, the new art form, was going to be called personality radio. My personality was going to be broadcast from 10 P.M. to 12 midnight on WABC.

> Hello again, here's my best to you.
> Are your skies all gray? I hope they're blue.

The first personality you'd hear on WABC in the morning wasn't talking, he was *singing*. His name was Herb Oscar Anderson, and he was known as the Morning Mayor of New York.

Morning men (and now women) are a strange and isolated lot. They rise at about 4 A.M. When they choose, as Herb did, to live a distance from their stations, they often have long, dark, dreary journeys to face before they arrive at a barren building that, at that time of day, is as silent as an empty warehouse. There they take in great quantities of caffeine and take on personalities not exactly their own in order to seem wide awake and on top of the still-slumbering world. They are truly self-starters, usually gregarious and confident. And, while their work hours cause them to peter out early, one has the sense that they know a good party when they see one. It was these people who, in the era of personality radio, set the tone of the radio day, taking whatever inspiration was available from the weather, the news wires, and deep inside themselves. Often they signed on after the station had been off for a number of hours. In major markets, they stretched and exercised a station into real-life reality after the yawning or manic overnight jock had held forth in the never-never land of predawn. All in all, it was and continues to be the kind of job only a strange early bird could love, but all across America people are as loyal to their morning radio show as they are to their spouses—sometimes more—and the morning people are usually the highest-paid, since they are the station's pacesetters.

In the sixties, the morning personality's job was even more difficult than it is today. This was the last gasp of the era when radio listeners were still viewed as one big pie, not demographic slices assigned to different formats. WABC generally believed it could appeal to anyone and everyone who had an AM radio. It particularly believed that to be true in the mornings. There will never be a more schizoid slot than the sixties mornings on that station. It was Herb's task to try to engender the loyalty of everybody within earshot of a 50,000 watt killer signal. He was supposed to appeal to the little old ladies brewing tea and deciding if they needed to call the beauty shop for a blue rinse; to the frantic mothers trying to get their seven-year-olds off to school before they killed their two-year-old siblings; to the dads who were on their way to the wired world of Wall Street, the madness of Madison Avenue, or the boxlike, boxed-in factories of New Jersey; and, above all, to the teen queens adjusting their fuzzy collars and poodle skirts, as well as to their manly counterparts lacquering their D.A. haircuts into submission.

No wonder Herb opened the show and came out of every top-of-the-hour newscast with that song. Better to be like Bing than Elvis if you're trying to appeal to the masses. It worked too. Herb even recorded his theme on the Columbia label.

Of course, the song took only about sixty seconds, so Mr.

Anderson still had to come across with some pleasing morning conversation. He'd tell the girls they looked pretty this morning, or ask them to wear something bright because the weather was murky, always reminding the secretaries to bring their umbrellas, knowing they'd be going out to buy nylons on their lunch hours and wanting to make sure they didn't ruin their hairstyles in the rain. His was the clear, sweet sound of someone who'd been born and bred in the Midwest. This was an uncomplicated man. People talked about "Squaresville" in 1961. The Morning Mayor of New York could surely have gotten elected ruler of that mythical hamlet. From 6 A.M. until 10 A.M., WABC's listeners heard a warm, harmless voice that was pleasant and unthreatening. In truth, they were hearing the voice of indifference. HOA, as Herb called himself, wasn't really there in the studio. He was absorbed in a magazine (usually from an agricultural supply house—it was his dream to return to a farm in Minnesota someday) or in the newspaper. Because the morning slot was such a powerful position, theoretically setting the radio dial for the whole day, Herb had a producer named Murray Barber who ran his show. When it came time for a commercial, Murray would hand Herb the copy and mention the name of the advertiser to him so he'd know who and what he was talking about, as in "Maxwell House, Herb. Coffee." Murray would also tell him the name of the record that was about to be played, cluing him in on the recording artist, just in case he was unfamiliar with the song, as in " 'Blue Moon,' Herb. The Marcels." Still, Herb managed to sound like your Uncle Herby, who was just fascinated by your biology assignment or your big basketball game on Saturday night, so his morning mayoralty was unimpeachable.

Many radio stations operate on a formula called dayparting. This simply recognizes that different kinds of people listen to the radio at different times of day. In the early sixties, it was widely assumed that after the men went to work, and before the kids came home from school, radio listeners were housewives and retirees. Because of this assumption, at 10 A.M. daily

WABC felt safe in going from its own personalities to that of Don McNeill in Chicago. Broadcasting live from the Allerton Hotel, McNeill's show was called the *Breakfast Club* and featured patter, interviews, swing music, and marches around the breakfast table to get the blood flowing—perfect radio for the geriatric set and the supposedly hair-curlered housewives who were around to listen to the radio at that hour, but deadly to the rock format. Why the parenthetical pause from the music that was fueling every successful station in America? WABC was part of the ABC radio network. More than that, WABC was the flagship station of the ABC radio network. There were network features and commitments that the flagship station was expected to wave the flag for. Square though he might be, Herb left no doubt that WABC understood what was happening in music. The *Breakfast Club*, on the other hand, left listeners wondering if WABC understood what was happening east of the Mississippi.

How to recover from that cyanide hour? With a guy who you could imagine telling dirty jokes at the Chamber of Commerce luncheon. His name was Charlie Greer. Straight out of Ohio, Charlie could have almost been a Breakfast Clubber himself. But he also was a perfect combination of down-home simplicity and big-city ambition that made the music of the sixties palatable to the older listeners still hanging in with the station and the young wives who were looking for company at midday.

"I was talking to my wife last night. You know my wife—Queen Kong," Charlie would start out, sharing with the listeners some wide-eyed observation on modern life. Then he would tell all the "Huggy Bears," as he called the members of his fan club, how wonderful the latest Shirelles release was, promising to play it right after we heard the "beautiful twin pianos of Ferrante and Teicher playing the magnificent 'Exodus.' " When I later moved to 7 to 11 P.M. and Charlie got the shift after mine, his casual midwestern approach to life in general became a casual approach to arriving at the studio on time. I then became less tolerant of his sweet, simple sail through the world of broadcasting. But at midday he was pretty much a joy, and always ready to promote the lineup that was coming up.

What was coming up was unlike anything that had ever been on daytime radio—a disc jockey who understood the dilemma of late afternoons and evening drive time and forged himself into the solution to the problem—Dan Ingram. Consider 2 to 6 P.M.: The kids are home from school. They've been cooped up in the strait-jacketed rule-laden halls of learning for longer than they thought they could endure. At an age when the fifty minutes of Spanish class seems the duration and torture of the Inquisition itself, a teenager who's set loose from school comes home, turns on his radio, and wants to hear a rebel who understands. At the same time, the moms who are getting dinner together want something to save the day from the tedium that has gone before—the errands, the housework, the budget. And what's going on out in the streets and on the highways? Is hubby going to arrive home in a crummy mood? Mom wants the straight scoop from somebody who isn't going to try to jolly her out of her concerns. Add to this the guys who've had the proverbial "rough day at the office," or the rotten day on the assembly line, and you've got the evening drive time audience. What did these people have in common? Something else in control of their lives. School. Responsibilities. Bosses. What was Dan's answer to this common malady? A daily thumbing of his nose at authority. Irreverence was Dan Ingram's religion. A news story about fare increases on the subway and bus lines? Dan would suggest that the city council try working for a living and see how they felt about having to pay extra to be cooped up in the subway sweatboxes. A vote for Miss Rheingold? Dan could imagine sharing a few icy ones with this year's redheaded contestant. He called his listeners "kemosabe." He was the Lone Ranger going after justice and everybody in the audience was his trusty sidekick.

After the delight of Dan Ingram, the network got its mitts on the station again. An hour and fifteen minutes of news and features. More than anyone ever wanted to know about current events and cultural affairs, particularly when you were dying to hear Ernie K-Doe sing "Mother-in-Law." Fortunately, WABC had a smooth transition out of the news. Silk was sandpaper compared to the suave Scott Muni. Gravelly-voiced, poised, Scott was the dreamy date every woman wanted to be standing on the doorstep at 7 P.M., the cool guy every young man wanted to be. With his savvy way of talking, Scott let listeners know he was in the know. His show opened with an hour of Solid Gold. It was no easy task to keep that hour fresh, with only the narrow band of gold available so early in rock's history. Imagine the kind of guy who could make you feel like this was the first time you'd heard "Rock Around the Clock" called a golden oldie and you've got Scott Muni.

Ten P.M. to midnight was my corner of the world. Admittedly, I'd loved the earlier slot of my WINS days, but I was determined to make something of the hours that were mine and I had the feeling I could really forge something out of a time period when I'd be free of the scrutiny of management and sales types.

When my show ended, the time slot the radio industry calls "overnight" began. Overnight is a flaky time and it's been approached in dozens of ways by thousands of radio stations. At this time of night you're talking to the night shift, insomniacs, and people who the police expect to meet up with when the moon is full.

There's no way to control such an audience, and basically there are three choices—go with the format and hang on to whatever listeners you can, entertain the listeners, or provoke the listeners. Talk shows are popular overnight because they are theoretically entertaining and/or provoking.

Big Joe's Happiness Exchange was neither, but it *was* compelling. Yes, for a while I turned the mike over to a man named Big Joe Rosenfeld and ABC turned from big-city radio to small-town stuff. Big Joe opened his show with a kind of singsong chant, part Bible Belt minister and part snake-oil salesman:

"I don't want to be rich. . . . I can't be good looking.
All I want to be is happy. What do you want to be?
You do? Well, good! Because somebody cares!"

When listeners joined Big Joe's club—the *Happiness Exchange*—they got to bring people on the air to tell their sad stories. Once these heart-wrenching tales of woe were told, money would pour in and other listeners would open their homes to the homeless. Good Samaritans samaritized nightly on ABC, until Big Joe tried to find happiness importing and using air time to promote trinkets from Taiwan. Soon he was off the air.

ABC was only too happy to exchange the *Happiness Exchange* for the sound of Bob Lewis. Bob had a gimmick called the Divariable Veeblefurtzer, an imaginary time machine that cranked out oldies. With his arrival, WABC began to rock around the clock for real.

This was my work family, my career home, my adult summer camp, my kid's fantasy of a trusty band of desperadoes.

I signed on my first show on ABC with "Maybelline" by Chuck Berry. It was the first song I had played when I got my own shift on WINS. I've started every new announcing stint with it and later used it to open each radio station I bought. Chuck recorded "Maybelline" in 1955 after the Chess brothers, Leonard and Phil, of Chess Records convinced him that the girl's name in the song he'd written should be something other than Ida Red. Where did Chuck get the name Maybelline? The story goes he took it from a children's tale he recalled. It was about a cow. Typical. One of the rock giants, Johnny B. Goode himself, launched his career with a song about a cow. More proof that anything could happen in the new music business, and all the more reason for it to be my official launch song—not to mention that it had a killer beat. I was on the air on WABC.

A month after I got to WABC, the station teamed up with the mayor's office for a "stay in school" campaign. The whole world thinks of New York as the Big City, but in 1961 citizens of Gotham often behaved as if it were a small town, trying to help solve the city's problems with community-minded actions. We fully expected to have an impact on the kids who saw a high school diploma as a ticket to nowhere. "Don't Drop Out" was the battle cry and the major event of this war against educational dropsy was the "Stay in School Spectacular" at the New York Coliseum. All the Swinging Seven Gentlemen were there—plus one. In 1961, WABC had run a contest called "The Star Search." They'd searched for the recording and radio greats of tomorrow, and the young, aspiring deejay they'd discovered turned out to be genuine star material. He was nineteen-year-old Les Marshak, who grew up to be one of the most admired and most talented voice-over announcers in the business. Anyone who's watched the Tony Awards on television, or any event on NBC Sports, has heard that commanding, compelling voice. It's the voice of a man who is both warm and powerful. His commercial work is the definition of professional and his status as my best friend doesn't have anything to do with that opinion, a consensus of the toughest ad and broadcasting people in the land.

As a nineteen-year-old, all of this was ahead of Les. He was simply a Columbia University pharmacy school student who loved radio. He was onstage at the Coliseum for that Stay in School Spectacular, wearing a red WABC sport jacket just like the big guys. Reminiscing, Les recalls that the crowd was excited when Bruce Morrow was introduced, yelling, "Welcome Back, Cousin Brucie!" After a year of exile in Miami, I had gotten back to New York wondering how long it would take to get back in the consciousness of the New York audience. That appearance just weeks after my WABC debut took away a great deal of insecurity. My cousins remembered me. What had been abruptly ended at WINS hadn't been an ending after all.

Experts say the first baby boomer was born just after midnight on January 1, 1946. That baby was fifteen years old when I got to WABC in 1961 and millions of other teenagers were boomin' and bloomin' all over the country. It was a teen scene. Rock was a teen sound. ABC was going after teen power and yours truly was in the late-night teen slot. If the early days of my ABC career were going to polish my style, this time slot was the perfect place to shine up my act. No news was the good news.

ABC had a big news commitment. No matter how strongly we felt about the music, we couldn't afford to screw around with the radio's sacred responsibility to broadcast news. By 10 P.M., though, the day's major news stories had been played out. There were no late-breaking developments from Washington or even the West Coast. Europe was deep asleep. What happened during the day had probably been heard on earlier radio broadcasts or from Uncle Walter Cronkite. Because of this, my show was pretty much free from the solemnity lent by the weight of world affairs. It's a lot easier to be breezy when you don't have to deal with politicians' hot air.

News broadcasts between 10 P.M. and midnight were pretty much local things or, for significant world impact, the score of the Yankees–Red Sox game. In this atmosphere it was appropriate to be silly. Besides, I'll always go for the tickle over the itch; I'm not really very interested in highbrow discussions when there's a chance to act like one of the Three Stooges instead. Furthermore, 10 to midnight is a punchy time, especially after a full day of acting basically like an adult.

If I'd been an overnight or morning jock, I would have had to be serious about when I slept and when I rose. Instead, I led two lives. I got up at about eight in the morning, was a family man, did appearances and business things during the day, checked out the fan mail, did free-lance commercials, played on the beach in the summer, and then at around six I got to the station and took care of whatever production work I had— commercials that I was supposed to record, station promos that were going to use my voice. By the time I went on the air, I was usually starting to get into that flaky state you feel when you're a kid and you're up past your bedtime. My brain probably said something like, "Oh yeah, we've got a show to do—better send some adrenaline out to keep the machine running." By the time my jingle went on the air, I was wired.

I helped the craziness along by staying just an inch away from pandemonium in the studio. Initially the ABC studios were set up so the engineers were in a soundproof room, separate from the air studio. There they worked the control panels that determined what went out over the air—the jock's microphone, the cartridge machines, used for playing recorded commercials and most songs (which were transferred from records to cartridge tapes to avoid the noise of scratched vinyl), the turntables that were used occasionally. The control panels had sliding volume controls called "pots" (potentiometers)—and the various network feed lines as well. *Star Trek* got some of its inspiration for the *Enterprise* spacecraft controls from inside a radio studio, obviously. When a commercial required a "live tag," an engineer would have to open a deejay's mike at the end of a recorded spot to allow for a piece of timely information: "And you'd better hurry to Gimbels to get in on the super lingerie sale. It lasts only two more days, ladies" or "And be sure and tell them Cousin Brucie sent you and you'll get a free soft drink with every hamburger you order." Air personalities and engineers usually communicated by pressing a "squawk button." I loved to hit the button while my mike was on, giving Saul, George, or Bob a chance to be a star. These guys had great instincts for timing and could feel the pace of the show. They also spent hour upon hour studying the techniques of the guys they engineered for. Given the chance, they got off some terrific one-liners.

Periodically I'd play the panic game. I'd slip under the console table while the engineer's back was turned. Swiveling back to give me a cue to read a commercial or introduce the next record, he would be faced with an empty broadcast booth. This is radio hell. George would prepare to cut to the record without an intro or to skip the commercial until I could be located (God, what if he's had a heart attack and is dying in the studio?). At the last second, I'd pop up, grinning, calmly ready to take the mike, and prepared to take like a man whatever retaliation was sure to come. I loved being tested to see if I could keep my cool.

What tests they were. I'd take the script for a live commercial from the looseleaf notebook, holding it at eye level in order to project my voice directly at the mike, just as students of broadcasting are taught. Stealthily, imperceptibly, the former victim of Morrow mischief would creep close, visible out of the corner of my eye. Honor-bound by the unspoken radio code to continue reading the spot, I'd concentrate hard on my delivery. The strike of a match, the flame. The script was on fire. It was a race against time to read the spot before there was nothing left to read, always ending with "Boy, it's getting hot in here, cousins!"

Foldouts from *Playboy* magazine. Condoms filled with water and sent blobbing across the studio like contraceptive jellyfish. These were the real tools of the engineer. There was no star system in those days at WABC—it was impossible to take yourself too seriously in an atmosphere that was part college dorm, part locker room.

Eventually, the station let the barrier down, putting jocks and engineers in one big studio. With that change, the management was acknowledging the value of interaction and, for me, it was practically sanctioning hysteria. If it was a slow night—no really great new hit tunes, quiet phones, maybe the night before a holiday or something—the engineer and I would line up deli ketchup and mustard packets on the counter that separated us. The game was called "dive bomber." The object was to close your eyes, raise your fist, and come down fast with a square hit on the end of one of the packets, forcing the contents to squirt out on your opponent. This took finesse. Come down on the wrong side of one of those envelopes and you'd shower yourself with condiment. Make too broad a hit and two packets could squish on you. Miss completely and you'd suffer humiliation. Your opponent was bound by gentleman's agreement to stand stoically as you took blind aim. If

I do say so myself, I became a master at deli war—and if in the telling it sounds childish, remember, child's play is what those days, that station, and my career were about.

These were the early days. Ten to midnight. Two hours when my primary audience was pretty much finished with TV and telephoning. I hear from now-grown-up women that they went to bed with me every night when they were young. Sounds great, but what they mean is they would finish their homework, set their hair on rollers or frozen-orange-juice cans, and turn off the lights. Either their parents allowed them to have the radio on, or they'd sneak a transistor under the covers. The dreamy songs would usher them to dream land while from the very center of Manhattan I would tell them life's great truths:

> "You're looking very alluring tonight, my darlings. I want you to go to sleep thinking beautiful thoughts. Think about this summer, being with somebody special . . . kissing, hugging . . . mmmmmmm. Now I have a perfect song for you . . . sweet dreams . . ."

Next door, across town, or far away, a dreamboat boy was listening too. The times were simple and the songs were simple ones. The jock named Cousin Brucie was the guy who stayed awake till they fell asleep. Long after they had to relinquish the phone for the night I was carrying messages between them. I was theirs—their courier, their night guide:

> "This song goes out to Danny in Union, New Jersey, from Cindy in Elizabeth. Cindy loves you, Danny, you dreamboat."

Bryan Hyland would sing "Sealed with a Kiss" and Cindy and Danny would symbolically kiss each other good-night.

So a night would end for two kids and so an era began for a radio station. A station with a destiny, and a life of its own, in a time that was unbelievably charged with possibilities. Nobody knew what was about to happen with WABC. What happened was truly a chemical reaction. The times, the people, the music, the station, all came together to create something bigger than the sum of its parts.

This isn't to say that WABC was a haphazard happening that didn't have a sense of direction. Hal Neal was a marine-sergeant type and a strong hand at the helm. Hal had brought a man named Mike Joseph in as a consultant to develop the broad early ABC format.

The Mike Joseph ABC format was based on the 770 dial position. The long playlist had seventy singles and seven hit albums. There were also seven Soaring Singles (songs that were going to be hits). In those days records were being turned out faster than doughnuts, and singles became part of albums rather than the other way around, so it wasn't hard to come up with dozens of songs to play during any given radio day. It seemed as though we had hits hourly, unlike today, when songs take longer to make the charts and linger there longer once they do.

That initial setting of the format was the sum of the structure in the early WABC days. There simply were no rules, because things were happening too fast and too wonderfully for rules. Never had this much music been loved by this many teenagers before. Never had teenagers been viewed as this powerful before. Never had corporate success come from something as seemingly spontaneous as rock music. There was no real precedent for dealing with bombastic broadcasting. Nobody knew what the rules should be so we flew by the seats of our pants. Listeners sensed the spontaneity of the station and loved it.

Hal Neal actually did have one rule: have fun. He had one goal too: number one.

In late 1961, after the September ratings came out, Neal called the Swinging Seven together (thankfully, and appropriately, the "Gentlemen" part of our team name had quietly disappeared) and told us the ratings had to go up. He'd told the big brass that we could carve a place for ourselves in New York rock radio and in the attendant advertising revenues, and he meant to deliver on his promise.

"I've got a deal for you," Neal said. "The first guy who becomes number one in his time slot gets a hundred and fifty dollars in cash and a new suit from Phil Kronfeld's store."

He didn't tell us how he wanted us to do it, he just told us he knew we could. Motivated by greed and bonded by the competitive instincts that had brought us to big-city radio in the first place, all seven of us went into on-air overdrive, creating extra shtick by coming in early and recording sound effects and other bits of audio energy, not sophisticated, but contributing to a sense of the unpredictable and wild atmosphere that teens craved.

> "I think we'd better call the mayor and ask him about the number of snow days left in the school schedule. We've got snow predicted for tomorrow and we want to make sure the Board of Ed has this thing organized. Let's see, Gracie Mansion . . ." [SOUND OF PHONE BEING DIALED] "The Mayor's Residence." "May I speak with the mayor? This is Cousin Brucie calling." [PAUSE] "He'll be right with you." [PAUSE] "He'll be right with us . . . we'll get this snow-day confusion straightened out. I wonder where he is . . ." [MAYOR SPEAKS AND SOUNDS A LOT LIKE BRUCE:] "Snow days? Snow days? Take a few of them off this week. Sure!"

The techniques may have been primitive, the humor may have been sophomoric, but the result was gorgeous. We didn't just carve a place for ourselves in the New York market, we made mincemeat of it. One month later, Neal called us together again.

"A hundred and fifty bucks and a new suit is going to . . . every one of you!"

That legendary air force had all made number one at the same time. We each got a new trench coat as a bonus.

In mid-eighties terms, $150 would be worth about $800, and although virtually every radio station in the country, then and now, gives commercial time to sponsors in return for goods and services to be given as prizes to listeners and perks to staff, that bonus, suit, and trench coat made me feel as though the station had spent a fortune on me.

In May 1961, America joined together to listen to a broadcast unlike any they'd ever heard before. It was piped into schoolrooms and service stations and hospital cafeterias and boardrooms. It started with the voices of "Mission Control" in Cape Canaveral, Florida, and hit a crescendo with the countdown to launching Alan Shepard into suborbital space flight. For seventeen minutes, Commander Shepard held us rapt with a riveting report of an uneventful exercise in technology.

It wasn't strictly coincidence that rock radio co-opted the jargon of NASA, talking of blasts, rockets, stars, and soaring. Like those fighter pilots, early rock jocks were cowboys, with a cocky swagger that belied our uncertainty about our ability to pull through in the unexpected situations we were facing for the first time in our industry's history. At WABC, ours wasn't a dangerous mission, but we were in the business of traveling uncharted territory.

Cool as Chuck Yeager radioing in an account of breaking the sound barrier, we pretended we knew what to expect even though most of the time we didn't. The country had a new frontier and we were on it every day, urban cowboy pilots with very little power over a tremendous force that was giving us the ride of our lives.

CHAPTER EIGHT

Down at Palisades Park

By the late fifties, America had discovered something wonderful. It was called leisure time. We no longer had to collect tin or animal fat in tin cans, volunteer at the Red Cross, or keep the war effort going. We were through working overtime to get a big enough nest egg so that we could afford to marry and have kids. Companies were offering "benefits" now, and unions were negotiating for extra vacation time and days off. We could work a forty-hour week and enjoy some time with the families we'd spent the beginning of the decade trying to afford. With the discovery of leisure time came the industries devoted to helping America's citizens spend its leisure-time budget. A man named Disney dreamed up a park that went beyond amusement—it was a whole world of fun, a clean, safe world where dreams really did come true. All around the nation, demi-Disneys had their own versions of family lands. One of these places was in New Jersey. It was called Palisades Park, and while it didn't have any super-colossal rides or wonderfully beautiful landscapes, it did have a signature attraction: rock 'n' roll. By 1962 Cousin Brucie was appearing there every Saturday and Sunday from the first weekend in April until the middle of September.

For a rock artist in the early sixties, being booked at Palisades Park was like boarding one of those rockets the rock jocks talked about. Once that influential New York metropolitan audience got a look at the acts, they adopted them. They bought their records, they followed their careers, they made them stars. To play Palisades was to enter a garden of fans there for the picking—fans whose loyalty was ensured *because* of the simplicity of the park, not in spite of it. This unpretentious place attracted unpretentious people. For the most part, the crowd was made up of solid middle-class families, out for a day they could afford in a place that was safe, clean, and fun for the Clearasil kids who were threatening to leave the nest at any moment. The crowd included teens on "safe" daytime dates, nineteen-year-old newlyweds who'd made out to Murray's submarine races or my "Love Hour Half Hours" on Saturday nights, and the occasional older brother or sister shepherding a carload of preteens down from Connecticut. These were not jaded pleasure seekers apt to be fickle in their choice of idols. These were simple folk, easily impressed, pleased, and won over. Give them a good performance, and they'd buy every 45 you put out.

It was at Palisades that Cousin Brucie got a face. By 1962, when I was in front of the Palisades audience every weekend of the spring and summer, I began to be recognized before I opened my mouth, a heady experience for a twenty-six-year-old who had been waiting for the recognition that was his just desserts since his caveman debut at James Madison High. Given the seduction of such recognition, the addiction potential of Palisades Park was high for me. Like the junk food it served, the park became a craving for the kid who used to spend his last quarter on Nathan's fries. Like all addictives, Palisades had a pusher. His name was Irving Rosenthal.

Mr. Rosenthal, owner of Palisades Park and giant of the

amusement industry, was about five feet tall. He was part Peter Pan, part Tom Sawyer, and part Ingrid Bergman in *The Bells of St. Mary's*. In other words, he was a master at getting people to do what he wanted. He was the last of the great carny men, that rare breed that created excitement out of canvas and plywood and America's love of playgrounds. Every March, when Irving and I would meet to discuss the upcoming Palisades season, he'd say, "You make sure you tell them, Brucie—millions of dollars' worth of new rides. Lights that could stretch from here to California. More attractions than ever before!" In truth, he'd whitewashed the food stands, changed the burnt-out bulbs, and leased space to a new ride broker who was replacing last year's Tilt-a-Whirl with the one Palisades had returned to another ride broker the year before. In Irving's eyes that was millions of dollars' worth of renovation and Irving's eyes were what counted, since it was his vision that built the money machine on the shores of the Hudson River. His was the vision of a man who mixed prowess with prejudice and had just enough power to make it pay off. For instance, Irving believed it was good for business to have a staff of workers who were reliable and stable, not the kind that would cause problems with constant turnover or demands. So he hired senior citizens to do all the jobs in the park that didn't involve hard physical labor. The juxtaposition of the gray-haired ticket takers with the kids who were waiting to ride one scream machine or another was a charming, if cockeyed, sight. It also created the family atmosphere that was more typically Maine or Michigan than the quick-buck world of New York metropolitan area recreation, and unlike the many parks manned by an ever-changing population of high school and college kids from year to year, Palisades Park visitors got to know the park employees, so going back every season was like going back to a camp where the counselors never changed. Thus had Mr. Rosenthal unwittingly profited doubly from hiring pensioners who didn't want to garner too much salary and lose their Social Security benefits. By providing a way for the oldsters to "keep busy" during the balmy days of April through September, he'd provided the park with a stability and grandmom-and-pop-ness that had far more panache than the palatial plastic parks of today.

It takes a kind of genius to have the instincts that breed good fortune, and that streetwise munchkin had that genius in spades. Convincing WABC that exposing their nighttime jock meant great exposure for the station and convincing me that spending my spare time booking acts from the steamy "office" he gave me in the bowels of the park was good for my career (since the better the acts the bigger the audience, and the bigger the audience the better for me), Irving sat back and let us promote his park. Playing Palisades became a coup for rock groups, and once again Irving was right when he said, "They're dying to appear at Palisades, Bruce. It's good for their records and when you talk about them in my commercials, they get a million bucks in free advertising."

Free advertising. Another Rosenthal specialty. Virtually every radio spot and newspaper ad that ever ran for Palisades Park was subsidized by a soft-drink or beer company, or a manufacturer of soapsuds (you could sometimes get into the park free if you brought a detergent box top with you), or even mass transportation.

> Skip the bother. Skip the fuss.
> Take a Public Service Bus.
> Public Service sure is great.
> Takes you right up to the gate!

This is a perfect example of the Rosenthal method of advertising. Citing the need to promote bus riding during off-peak weekend hours, Irving convinced the Public Service Bus Company to promote its Palisades Park line on the Cousin Brucie show since "all the kids listen to the guy and he'd be great talking about buses!" Public Service signed up for a hefty advertising schedule, all promoting Palisades Park, at no expense to the park's owner.

Still, for all his finagling, Irving was something of a lovable, dizzy Disney. He was a Damon Runyon character, handing the Four Seasons chits for rides and kewpie dolls for their girl-friends and kids. He had promotion in his soul, so everybody from the wrestler Antonino Rocca to Hollywood heartthrob Michael Callan to one-time guest Clint Eastwood (plugging his *Rawhide* TV show) was encouraged to "go, enjoy yourself, ride the rides . . . eat."

Of course, a colorful character needs some colorful eccentric-ities, and Irving had a doozy: He was afraid of the roller coaster. He absolutely forbade any of the performers to go near it. He may not even have minded if the paying public stayed away. Naturally, this made the thing all the more appealing to me. A weekend hardly went by without a sneak ride on Rosenthal's nemesis.

"Brucie," he'd whine, when he caught me, "Brucie, please don't do this to me. Stay off that contraption. It makes me nervous. Play the games. Ride the merry-go-round. Eat! Some-body give Brucie a coupon to have a steak in the restaurant. Here, have a Coke. Just stay away from that thing!"

I was Irving's protégé, his resident "celebrity," part crazy entertainer, part son. If I gave him every spring and summer weekend for the better part of a decade, he gave me something far greater. He gave me a playground, and a chance to further my career while essentially still playing on the makeshift stages of Barbara's garage and around the campfire at Camp Swago. At Palisades, I was the kid on East Twenty-sixth. Nothing was really different from those days, except the size of my audience and the names of the entertainers. Where once I had offered Popeye, I was now offering Tony Bennett. Where once the kids had lollygagged along to Barbara's garage, there were now crowds that gathered at ten in the morning, hoping for a rickety seat in the amphitheater, but willing to stand for some or all of the three-hour stage show, holding signs that said things like PARAMUS LOVES COUSIN BRUCIE! or WABC IS THE GREATEST, or the inevitable SOMEPLACE HIGH SCHOOL. STATE CHAMPS 1963.

On the day Mr. Bennett came to the park, Irving's "careful" spending policies backfired. This was not the kind of place where one found a thirty-piece orchestra (or even a piano on most days). This was the land of lip-syncing. This meant that under the stage were two guys sweating in the 120-degree oven that served as a "production studio." Their equipment consisted of a couple of turntables, barely electrified (Irving would have run them with mice in wheels if he could have produced enough power that way), and cables leading not to broadcast or concert speakers, but essentially public-address speakers. If they were good enough for announcements at poolside, they were good enough for piping music, was the philosophy. Bill Haley and His Comets lip-synced at Palisades (if the guys had really played their instruments there would have had to be a fee for the performance based on the codes of the musicians' union). Fabian, Frankie Avalon, Bobby Rydell—graduates of the University of Lip-Sync, *American Bandstand*—mouthed the lyrics beautifully. The Shirelles shimmied to their records, smiling, gesturing, silent, while from backstage, "Soldier Boy" was sent out to the adoring fans, happy to be seeing glamour so close, glad to hear the song *exactly* the way it sounded on the radio. But Tony Bennett? Tony Bennett could have sung "Rags to Riches" a cappella and had the crowd in the palm of his hand. Still, this *was* a radio audience, and radio with action was what we were giving them. So Tony mouthed leaving his heart in San Francisco, and about halfway through was stricken by that horrible evil that stalks any performer who's ever stood in front of an audience and pretended to be singing while a record was playing—the record skipped. And skipped.

"My love waits there in San Fran, San Fran . . . San Fran." Weak smile. Blush. A hand raised to the audience, a pleading look offstage, Tony Bennett, my mother's idol, had been embarrassed. What was I going to do about it?

"Ladies and gentlemen. Ladies and Gentlemen. A little technical difficulty there. Our engineers tell me that the equipment in Studio Three B is a little finicky-y today. Why don't we just have a chat while they're working on it, Tony? I hear you're going to be appearing in Las Vegas soon. It must be a lot like playing Palisades Park, being in Vegas . . ."

Ad-lib. Cover up. Punt. The audience loves you, kid, you can do no wrong. Just keep letting them know you love them back.

That was the secret, after all. We were in the last shining moment of audiences feeling loved. Not cloying sugar sincerity doled out with a false smile and a benevolent wave, but absolutely from the gut. There had come to be a very special kind of performing during the two wars that the world gave numbers to. And during World War II we at home saw newsreels of our most beloved performers entertaining the troops, bringing them the love that was waiting at home, letting them know that they were the most important people in the world. Palisades Park didn't happen all that long after those USO shows and I had learned my craft in part by watching those newsreels. Every week I was putting out a blend of USO show and hip sixties strutting. If these were the first rock fests, they were also the last love fests. The audience was not only loving the performers and loved by them in return, they were in love with each other.

They'd come over during a break in the show, hand in hand, eyes looking up and then shyly down. The girl would always talk first: "Hi, Cousin Brucie."

"Hello there. What's your name?"

"JoAnne."

"Well, hi, Cousin JoAnne. And who's this handsome guy with you?"

"Billy," he'd answer.

"He just gave me his ring, see?"

Hanging from the chain around her neck, clinking against a crucifix as likely as not, would be a chunky high school ring with a blue or red glass "stone." JoAnne would finger it, slide it on the chain, tilt her chin down to get a good look at it.

"Going steady. That's terrific. Come to my radio broadcast tonight and I'll put you on the air."

"Great! See ya."

See ya. See ya a dozen times a weekend. Going steady. Engaged. Just married. They'd come by to say hello and to tell their friend from the radio their good news. I dressed for the occasion. Looking like an usher at a rock wedding, in leopard-skin tux, iridescent green tux, or virtually anything the tailor in the Bronx who'd outfitted the groups at the Apollo theater cared to make for me, I'd strut that stage. The suits had matching shoes most of the time. The leopard-skin number had real leopard-skin shoes. The poor man's Liberace. An earlier Elton. A guy who brought his poodle along in matching outfits.

Yes, Muffin Morrow came along, and got quite a following. Fans would call during the week and ask how Muffin was doing, or what Muffin was planning to wear to Palisades on the coming weekend. Many of them were the owners of members of the Muffin Morrow fan club, an exclusive organization open only to members of the animal, fish, or fowl kingdoms. This was an organization that grew so quickly during the one Palisades summer when we promoted it on WABC that I had to hire a clerical service to fulfill the thousands of applications for membership.

They were simple, crazy times, yes. The kind of times when a record promoter named Chuck Barris could buttonhole the park owner on a Saturday night and tell him he had a great new song he'd written, "Palisades Park." Didn't Irving want to hear it? Of course he did. Barris played it for him in his office and I was summoned.

"Brucie, Brucie, listen to this. You've got to play it on your show tonight. Terrific, isn't it?"

It *had* the sound, that was for sure. And the tri-state area would love it. Freddie Cannon, who'd hit with "Tallahassee Lassie" and "Way Down Yonder in New Orleans," was a proven commodity. Only one problem. Nothing went on the air without Rick Sklar's approval. No problem for Mr. Rosenthal. A call to the program director's home with a reminder of all the free publicity the station got from Palisades Park, a play of the record with the receiver held to a speaker, and the OK was granted. Two weeks later "Palisades Park" was in the Top Ten nationwide.

A simpler time. Palisades Park was the definition of it. Our big productions ran to Prettiest Palisades Baby contests, twist contests, and the annual Miss Teenage Palisades Park Pageant. These events attracted parents as well as kids, and just as some of the early "rock" acts were crossover artists from the earlier world of adult music, the promotions crossed the lines of appeal between parents and their offspring. Rock was the venue of the young, yes, but back then there was room enough in the worlds that promoted rock for the whole family. Just minutes after Lesley Gore left the stage, sixteen sixty-year-old ladies would be up there vying for Palisades Grandmother of 1964.

"And where are you from, Mrs. Iancola?"

"White Plains."

"And *you're* a grandmom? I can't believe it. You look like my date to the Senior Prom!"

(GIGGLE) "I'm old enough to be your mother, Mr. Brucie."

"Don't call me mister. I'm your *cousin.* Now, tell me, how many grandbabies do you have? . . ."

With a live three-hour stage show on Saturday and another on Sunday, the excitement and the conversation sometimes wore a little thin, but the enthusiasm never did. Two three-hour shows a weekend, with Irving screaming at me from offstage, "That's it, end the show, end the show!" He'd checked the receipts at the food stands and rides and revenue wasn't high enough, he wanted those people roaming the park, but I wouldn't let them go. There were acts waiting to go on, after all. A four-hour live radio broadcast every Saturday night. A live TV show as Clay Cole's co-host in between. This was a typical summer weekend for me. Hey, we were an energetic country; we demanded such stamina from ourselves.

One weekend a month I did the show AWOL. I was in the air force reserve during those Palisades Park years, stationed at

Mitchell Air Force Base in Garden City, Long Island. I was able to be absent from those Saturdays when I was supposed to be being a soldier because I had a major who was a music fan. He pretended he didn't know I was sneaking out and I pretended I was getting away with something, but since everybody had seen and heard the ads about my appearance all week long and since everybody in the unit listened to the live broadcasts, it was clear I wasn't getting away with anything. What I was getting was great at changing my clothes while driving. On Saturday mornings I'd leave the barracks wearing my uniform. I'd get into my car and drive like a maniac, stripping at every red light. By the time I reached the George Washington Bridge I'd be wearing my outrageous onstage garb. Meanwhile, at the park, my dad and my brother, Bob, would be getting Muffin into costume and warming up the audience. I can't count the number of times I arrived just as the show was about to begin. Irving finally lost patience. "Let me call up the president and tell him you should be out of the air force!" he demanded. Not quite wired to the president, Irving did write his congressman, who, being from New Jersey, had little jurisdiction over the nation's military. Besides, I liked testing the air force to see if they'd look the other way for rock 'n' roll, and they did, every time.

Palisades Park was simply a place where everything was destined to work out fine. Our aspirations weren't greater than our capacities in those days. Though Hollywood sent us its Michael Callans and its Clint Eastwoods and the big labels sent us their biggest stars, we were still a sweet operation, giving the audience a chance to touch and be touched, not keeping them at arm's length.

The closest we came to extravaganza was in the hands of a lady named Ross. Here was glamour in motion. Diana Ross was trailed by a cadre of hairdressers, wardrobe mistresses, secretaries, and support staff. Together with the Supremes she was to perform one song on tape for the *Mod Mod World* show I was producing and hosting from London and the States. We

127

started the taping after the park closed at eleven. At five the next morning we were still at it. A take that looked perfect to me and to the crew was missing something, in Diana's judgment. It would be done again, tighter, with the most subtle changes—the look in her eyes when the camera closed in, the angle of her wrist during the carefully choreographed chorus, the way the girls closed in to their mikes when they backed her up. Each and every detail of that two and a half minutes of tape was scrutinized and simonized. It had to be polished perfection or it couldn't go out as Diana Ross and the Supremes. Watching her, fading fast between takes, I'd go over and say, "Terrific, Diana, terrific, girls, so tell me, what are the Supremes up to?"

I knew Palisades was prologue for this lady. "She puts the awe in the audience"—those were the words that came to me that night. Not yet thirty, but an old man of the radio business, I was thankful to be awed.

Did we awe the hundreds of thousands who passed through those gates high above the Hudson during the era that was Palisades Park? In a funny way we did. We awed them in their memories. I have yet to do an appearance without someone coming up and saying to me, "Remember those days at Palisades Park?" Seen from the present, looking through that long tunnel to the past, Palisades seems awesomely simple, unbelievably dear, a hometown fair where the greatest luminaries imaginable stopped by. The carnival barker was a guy in a leopard-skin tux who strode, mike in hand, with an impertinent poodle scampering behind. He'd twist with Chubby or wrestle with Antonino. He'd crown Miss Teenage Palisades or the Grandmother of the Year. He'd put JoAnne and Billy on the air the night she got his ring and he'd wave to them when they were back next summer. A tall guy, but not the least bit larger than life. Life fit me perfectly in those days. I didn't want to be anything but life-size, nor did I need to be.

CHAPTER NINE

Radio Was Your Friend

April 4, 1964. Cousin Brucie, that unflappable, cool radio personality was flapped. I was pacing the waiting room of Doctors Hospital in Manhattan. Somewhere inside that mysterious maze, Susan was about to give birth to our first child. I was going to be Cousin Daddy!

What was a guy like me to do while waiting for his first child to be born? In 1964, fathers were as likely to help with the delivery as they were to help with diapering the baby once it got home (Desi never helped Lucy, remember). I wasn't used to being shut out of a performance. Either I was center stage or in the wings waiting to introduce an act. What exactly was my role here and who was the audience?

I needed help coping with this one, but who to call on? I had it. I'd call Dan. Dan had a bunch of kids; he could keep me calm. Besides, he was on the air, in perfect control—just the tone I needed to hear.

"Studio."

I was through on the private line and Dan was in broadcast mode, curt, distracted, when the word got through.

"Dan, it's me, Bruce. I'm at the hospital. This is taking forever. What's going on there?"

Dan wasn't about to soothe me with idle chitchat though. I'd touted the arrival of this kid as if it were the Second Coming, the Dodgers returning to Brooklyn, and New Year's Eve rolled into one. My buddy Mr. Ingram didn't mind catching me a little nervous after I'd milked my impending fatherhood so shamelessly.

"Hey Bruce, let me put you on the air. The listeners will love this!"

"Dan, it's kind of private. I don't have anything to say, really . . ."

"Listen, kemosabes. Guess what's going on at Doctors Hospital? Cousin Brucie is about to become a father. Let's get an update. How's it going, Brucie?"

Expectant father goes into air personality overdrive:

"Well, Dan, the big moment is almost here. The doctor says my son is going to be born soon. I'm just standing by here at the hospital waiting to hear him broadcast his first cry."

"How do you know it's a boy, Bruce?"

"I ordered one, Dan."

"I should have known. Keep us posted on the little cousin's progress into the world, will you, Brucie?"

"I sure will. In the meantime, dedicate a song to the doctors and nurses at Doctors Hospital for me, Dan. I'm going to go wash up now in case they need any help."

Wash up in case they need help? Keep them posted? There were at least six closed doors and a staff of dozens between me and the action. What could I possibly have to keep the audience posted on? Give an overenergized deejay enough time alone in a Green Room with old *Field and Stream* magazines and he'll come up with something. I called in meaningless updates as if they were reports from the London Blitz. Every time a nurse came out to tell me things were going fine, I had a major bulletin for the listeners. Finally a doctor emerged.

"You have a son, Cousin Brucie."

"Doctor, thank you. I have a son. I have a son. Doctor, can I ask you something?"

"Certainly. What are you concerned about?"

"Is it all right if I call WABC and put you on the air right now?"

Show me a doctor (particularly an obstetrician) and I'll show you Laurence Olivier. My son's usher into the world wasn't a bit shy. He went on and regaled the greater tri-state area with a stirring account of what amounted to a very routine delivery. Ben Casey couldn't have been more dramatic. I wasn't about to be upstaged, though. I had an ace up my sleeve.

"I want the listeners to know that Susan and I already have a name picked out. My son is going to be named Dana Jon— D.J."

I'm not sure what would have happened if I'd named him George or Aloysius, but I know what happened when we called him D.J. The fans felt like he was theirs. Thirty thousand cards, letters, and gifts came to the studio, the hospital, the house. Bags of letters were everywhere, and let me tell you something you may not know—mail stinks! Put enough sacks of mail in a closed space and you get an odor that pretty much approaches the brown-paper-bag aroma of a high school cafeteria mixed with the scent of a major league locker room. Luckily I had a way of dealing with this overwhelming outpouring of good wishes. I shipped it to my parents' basement. They'd helped me answer every piece of mail since the early WINS days. By now they were my official "answering service." Popping with pride over their grandson, they were in the incomprehensibly sweet position of being the recipients of a congratulatory flood from total strangers who seemed to be as convinced of Dana Jon's singularity as his grandparents were. I'll admit it wasn't all generosity that inspired me to give them the baby's first correspondence. It was a convenient way of keeping Mina and Abe occupied on East Twenty-ninth Street so they wouldn't spend every waking minute at our place hovering over the new Morrow Messiah.

We got booties and sweaters and monogrammed ceramic plates. There were cakes and cookies, rattles and teething rings. Dana Jon started his life with enough merchandise to open Kids Я Us. And, in fact, the boy who went on to be an MIT graduate was probably smart enough to do that by the time he was out of diapers (a little fatherly pride), but instead he's decided to become a doctor. He's studying at McGill University medical school now, but had he decided to, he could have been a great radio personality. Jon went on the air when he was three years old and made almost as many public appearances as I did between 1966 and 1976. Sometime around age twelve, he decided show biz wasn't challenging enough for him and turned his talents to studying French and exploring the world of science, building rockets and nuclear weapons in his bedroom. By that time, my darlings Paige and Meri had brought the number of my offspring to three. The girls are more stage-oriented than their adored older brother and it will surprise me not at all if, with their great beauty and flair for the dramatic, one or both of them gives Meryl Streep a run for her Oscar money.

My son was born on the air. Mick Jagger and Jerry Hall use Secret Service tactics to guard their privacy during the birth of a child. In a lighthearted attempt at anonymity, Christie Brinkley wore Groucho glasses when she left the hospital with the daughter she and Billy Joel were blessed with. I know my status as a celebrity doesn't approach that of the aforementioned, but I wasn't exactly chopped liver and crowds had been known to gather.

So why did I practically broadcast from the delivery room? I didn't relish the possibility of a mob scene when we left the hospital (actually, it was a small gathering of buoyant well-wishers), but there wasn't any question that I would share the moment with the listeners. Accessibility was what personality radio meant to me. You touched the fans and they touched you. The birth of a child is the ultimate family event. WABC radio was nothing if it wasn't a real part of the family, unlike our television counterpart, which had about as much to do with real families as *Get Smart* had to do with the CIA.

On TV we had *The Donna Reed Show* and *Father Knows Best*—picture-perfect families where nobody drank, nobody lost a job, nobody got a pimple, and the biggest trauma was whether Mom could hide from Dad the new hat she'd bought out of the grocery budget. On *My Three Sons,* Steve Douglas was the easygoing widower who could always talk through his kids' problems with them, and share his own in the process—group therapy in a white-frame house. Real life was something closer to *Rambo Comes to Dinner*. Take a household with one or more teenagers and you've got war. Declared or undeclared, it's still war, as the nation of adults and the nation of adolescents clash over the territories of freedom and power.

WABC was the DMZ. In this land of music, patter, and contests promising to make you rich, famous, and happy forever, there could be peaceful coexistence. Mom and Dad might hate the "noise" we played, but they knew their kids were basically safe with us. On the air we were ageless, trustworthy baby-sitters and even if Dan did get a little out of hand now and then, you still knew he'd kill any guy who tried to lay a hand on your daughter. Kids, on the other hand, knew we really understood them. We realized the true value of the Four Seasons, and we probably had actually met Dion; we were in touch with the real world, unlike those wardens their parents had become.

Families came to us to mediate. They were as involved with WABC as they were with neighboring families, and they called on us the way they would have called on a neighbor.

Many times the distraught mothers and fathers of runaways would be on the dedication line. The story was always pretty much the same. Their son or daughter had left home a couple of days ago and the police thought the child had probably run away. Would I go on the air and ask him or her to come right home? The parents always seemed to be crippled by grief and worry, contrite over some argument that had turned into this event.

With the guidance of the New York City police department, an effective way of responding to runaway calls evolved. It began with a plea to the kid to call the studio if the parents had agreed to let me meet alone with the child before they came to the studio. Many kids couldn't make the long journey home without a stop in the middle. They needed to touch base with someone they could trust before they could trust home base again. The parents had to also agree not to punish the boy or girl, to talk things out instead.

"Billy or Joanie," the plea would go, "your mom and dad are very, very worried. The most important thing is that we know you're all right. I'm going to ask all the listeners to keep the lines open for half an hour. Call me here at WABC, and we'll talk about it. Your parents don't want to punish you. They just want to know you're all right. I won't tell them where you are, just let me hear from you. OK, Billy, just call and talk to your Cousin Brucie."

Very often they called and most of the time they'd come up to the studio. If they got that far they'd usually let me call their parents to come and get them.

Sometimes kids would refuse to let the parents come for them. They all let me place calls so they could at least talk. Most of the runaways would pass out of this hard time into a more peaceful part of puberty. Others would be on the outs with the world forever. I witnessed both touching reunions and hateful screaming matches. I saw the saddest, most frightened children, too young to feel like adults, but too old to be treated like babies. All of them seemed unsure of how they'd managed to do something so drastic, and were anxious for things to be all right again.

Sometimes the stories were even worse. If a child came in and said his parents beat him, or if he was one of the unfortunates who actually showed the heartbreaking bruises of parental abuse, the police would be called before the parents. Too afraid to know the real story, I'd let the wide-eyed or withdrawn youngster go, believing that the man in blue could make it better for him, hoping against hope that it would turn out to be a misunderstanding between the generations. Stories of child beating and teenage prostitution were the stuff of tabloids and magazines that didn't make their way into "nice" neighborhoods. Certainly you'd never see the subject approached in a television show, or even hinted at on the evening news. Didn't that happen in some part of the country where there wasn't running water or radio? For one disc jockey and most of America in the mid-sixties, it was better not to know the answer to that question, and thankfully it was a question that didn't present itself often.

Even kids in the mainstream strayed now and then. A scout master once called to say some cub scouts had wandered away from the pack in Bear Mountain State Park. They were lost in the cold mountain woods, but he knew they had transistor radios with them and if I'd tell them to play their radios very, very loud, he was sure he could find them.

Half an hour later the cubs were rescued.

"I'm going to kill myself, Cousin Brucie. I want to talk to you first. Can you talk to me for a minute? I'm going to do it, I just need a minute to talk first. Can you talk to me, Cousin Brucie?"

These were the calls that didn't feel like real life. These were the ones that brought the nerve endings right to the surface of the skin and sent the stomach leaping into the throat and quickly down to the kneecaps.

Pills or razor blades. These were the routes to relief from a place so intensely painful that there seemed no way to keep the person talking. Have the engineer segue records until I could get a phone number. Give the caller the numbers of the suicide help line and drug action centers.

Once a woman said no, I couldn't have anybody call her. No, she wouldn't call anybody. Nobody gave a damn about her. Nobody would help.

"I'll help you. The police will help you. What if the police came to take you to the hospital?"

"They won't come. Nobody ever comes."

"They'll come. I'll call them. Tell me your address. I'll stay on the phone with you until they get there."

"They won't come."

Finally she told me the address. We talked on the phone until the police arrived.

"We're here, Cousin Brucie," the patrolman said when he took the phone from her. "She's got about a dozen bottles of pills here, but she's going to be all right. We're on our way to Bellevue."

Cousin Brucie, not Bruce Morrow. Once again it was a radio personality who carried out my responsibility as a member of the family of man. Once again the microphone connected me to a part of life that made up the life of the community I was part of and a bigger world as well. It was a world and a time when disc jockeys were priests as well as carnival barkers. Nearby friends, not faraway stars.

CHAPTER TEN

The Promotion Machine

One way to find out what was going on in the sixties world was to pick up a large magazine with a red masthead and bold white letters: *Life*. Ah, how many times did one bemoan the cruel twists of fate only to have an unsympathetic listener say "What's Life? A magazine." *Life* was *the* magazine. A photography nut like the disc jockey who called himself Cousin devoured it for the sheer joy of seeing pictures that were worth tens of thousands of the words that were his stock in trade. I could spend a whole show enthusing about John Glenn's flight, but *Life* would capture the magnificence of the event in a black-and-white photo. The meaning of *Life* was also to document everyman with the drama and importance that other publications most often reserved for heads of state. If communication with ordinary people was my aspiration, portraying them was *Life*'s achievement. During the early sixties, *Life* often printed photographs of college students stuffing themselves into phone booths or swallowing goldfish. Volkswagen bugs were crammed with people the way tiny circus cars carried dozens of clowns. Where did this mania come from? Did the nation just naturally go crazy after a war? Did media attention create publicity stunts? Or were we maybe simply a country that loved to get together and do nutty things?

Whatever the answer, America's radio stations noticed the nation's love of a challenge and capitalized on it with crazy contest promotions. Instead of going to the state fair once a year, one could win prizes every day by tuning in on the AM band. WABC was to contest promotions what *Life* was to photography. By 1963, we had them down to an art form.

The biggest promotion in the history of WABC and probably the history of all radio was the Principal of the Year Contest—send in the name of the best school principal and stay tuned to see how your school is doing. In 1962, the first contest had produced three million ballots and a nun as the winner of a color television set. Those three million ballots were not from three million students. No, ABC had encouraged stuffing the ballot boxes. Have your family vote. Vote as many times as you like. Send in a vote in your baby sister's name. Like those phone booths, packing the mailboxes was a challenge. Of course, if your school wasn't mentioned on the air as a front-runner, you had to get busy and send in some more votes. Then you'd have to listen to see if your school was inching closer to fame, fortune, and greed. Meanwhile, since it was a rating period, if you'd gotten one of the Arbitron rating diaries you (or your parents, who loved contests that promoted education) would dutifully note that you were listening to 77 WABC. We'd become even more powerful, and to be named Principal of the Year on ABC would be even more meaningful. Such is the predictable progression of promotion.

By 1963, Principal of the Year was the Nobel Peace Prize of the scholastic set. Schools that had lost in the last election were pissed off. It didn't matter that the winner last year had been a nun. She was the enemy. Rick Sklar, who had joined WABC in June 1962 was hot to trot on this promotion. He was out to outpromo every other station in the city. Together we went on a helicopter tour of suburban high schools to hype the contest. From the West Side helipad we whirled into New Jersey, Connecticut, and Long Island, landing on football fields, rooftops, and, one time, in a principal's backyard.

Midway through the contest it had become clear that we were in over our heads. The streets literally were blocked by traffic delivering votes. Since accusations were flying that some schools were requiring kids to stay after school to write thousands and thousands of ballots, we shouldn't have been surprised to see school buses arriving with sacks of mail. Studios were filling with tons of paper. Sklar and the management decided to rent St. Nicholas Arena, just down the block from the studio, to hold the overflow. By the time the contest was over, 176 million ballots had been cast. The station spent a bundle to hire a staff of eighty for the two months it took to count the votes. Helen Hill, principal of Teaneck High School in New Jersey, was the winner and WABC was winning the undeclared contest to be the most amazing station ever.

The secret of how big it all got was, in a way, how small we thought. We weren't bigger than life; we were part of the life of the city. Principal of the Year was pretty small-town. It was just that our small town was primarily the three states that surrounded America's biggest city, a city that did things in a big way. This was the city that coaxed *Mona Lisa* out of the Louvre.

Even before Principal of the Year, *Mona* had put us on the promotion map when she came to the Metropolitan Museum of Art.

"Mona Lisa, Mona Lisa, men have named you," sang Nat King Cole. After this smooth intro, the recorded promo featured frantic Cousin Brucie exciting the listeners to the possibility of winning one hundred dollars! All you had to do was paint the best *Mona*, the worst *Mona*, the biggest, or the smallest.

Salvador Dali judged the entries. There were fifteen thousand of them. Fifteen thousand people and groups had taken the time to create paintings and WABC needed to display them so the great Dali could make his decision. The judging of the big pieces was held at the Polo Grounds. It was a windy, overcoat day and the artwork began to fly around. Luckily there was a supermarket nearby. Heavy boxes of detergent were brought in to weigh the paper down. Unluckily, the clouds got darker and darker and finally the rains came. The Polo Grounds filled with soapsuds and many a *Mona* floated on the sudsy sea, losing paint in the process.

Stalwart Salvador weathered the storm. In my eyes he defied it. Here was one of the monsters of modern art on a sports field, looking at amateur renditions of one of history's great masterpieces. His dignity was uncompromised and even the blanket of bubbles couldn't diminish it. "This is quite good," he'd pronounce. "Not bad. This is rubbish . . . remove it." I became a fan on the spot. My art collecting had been confined to that one creepy experience at Mel Leeds's wife's gallery, but I knew someday I had to own a Dali. And one day I finally did. When I bought my first radio station, the Dali was one of the first things I brought in. That station was housed in an old armory that looked like a castle and it seemed fitting that it would be home for the man who strode like a king through what could have been a humbling experience.

"Stop by a participating McDonald's restaurant TO-DAY! Get your twenty-five-thousand-dollar button and pin it on! You might be the lucky listener who wins . . . twenty . . . five . . . thousand . . . dollars, dollars, dollars!"

Echo-chambered, shouted, dramatized, these words were heard about six times an hour. Millions of WABC listeners walked the streets wearing their orange buttons, hoping for one of the thousands of instant cash prizes or the grand prize of twenty-five big ones. The value of the advertising that button provided was worth dozens of times more than $25,000. Millions of people wearing the WABC logo on their lapels, hats, pocketbooks, diapers, added up to a gigantic presence for the station. And, since WABC handled every promotion to the letter and spirit of the law, listeners knew that the prizes and payoffs were real and really would be awarded. The "$25,000 Button" was a relatively simple contest idea—requiring only a sponsor of the magnitude of McDonald's to underwrite millions of buttons in return for being the exclusive outlet for obtaining them. WABC was such a force by that time that a contest didn't need to be elaborate to create interest. By 1964, we weren't scrambling for listener participation, we were assuming it—a luxurious position indeed.

Which isn't to say we didn't hit a snag now and then. One day on our way to lunch, Rick and I spotted some kites flying from the roof of a Japanese restaurant. We commented on how great kites were and how they were having a resurgence during the flower-power time we were living in. One thing led to another and by the time the lunch was over, the Great WABC Kite Contest had been born.

Later in the day, a recorded promo was on the air:

> "One hundred dollars for the biggest kite! One hundred dollars for the smallest kite! One hundred dollars for the most beautiful kite! Make a kite and fly it in the Sheep Meadow in Central Park at ten o'clock this Saturday. Cousin Brucie is going to be there to give away hundred-dollar bills to lots of lucky listeners. This contest has no strings attached. Be there!

Simple enough, eh? All I had to do was spend about an hour in Central Park on a Saturday morning and hand out some cash. No big deal. Unless you happen to underestimate the enthusiasm of the listeners. Blithely, on a sunny spring day, Rick and I strode to Central Park, a couple of radio guys who were on top of the world. We'd called a happening in the biggest park in the country's biggest city and now were on our way to survey what a happy little happening it would be. And

141

so we learned about creating a monster. As we approached the park, the sky grew dark. Would this be another *Mona Lisa* nightmare? No, the overcast was not cloud-inspired—there was a kite eclipse in progress. There were thousands of kites in the heavens and thousands of people attached to them on the ground. We walked into a sea of outstretched arms, string, frolicking children, and barking dogs. Rick and I looked at each other, knowing full well that we should have had at least a dozen judges for this one. We decided we'd punt.

Dizzily stumbling through the crowd, looking like drunken puppets attached to some great puppeteer above, the two blasé guys who only minutes ago had been congratulating themselves on their great promotional prowess were now close to panic. Pretty soon the crowd got restless. It was clear to them that their kites weren't exactly getting a fair shake. We sped up the judging. Smallest kite was easy—a postage stamp–size beauty with the WABC logo all over it in minute script. Biggest was easy too. The life-size replica of the Wright Brothers' plane took that one. The judgment calls—most beautiful, most original, and so forth, were made on the fly as Rick and I ran for our lives from the masses that could have gotten ugly at any time. I could imagine our colleagues from the news side of WABC giving a bulletin: "We have some tragic news from Central Park. Our own program manager, Rick Sklar, and air personality Bruce Morrow were trampled to death in Central Park this morning. The two broadcasters who had the world on a string only yesterday were sacrificed in a kite-contest promotion. Stay tuned for more details."

We learned our lesson. Never underestimate the power of WABC or the energy of our listeners. This lesson would be borne out again and again, but never so dramatically as the night I opened the phones to the seventy-seventh lucky caller. The prize was two tickets to a Beatles concert.

The phone lines connecting Manhattan with Queens, Brooklyn, and Staten Island blew. Service was restored after the phone company determined where the problem had originated. The next day the WABC brass were visited by phone-company honchos. Did they realize that it was within the phone company's authority to legally remove all of the telephones from the WABC studios? Did they understand they had endangered the lives of the citizens of Manhattan for . . . for . . . for concert tickets?! Did it ever occur to them that a phone circuit can handle only so many calls? Didn't they foresee the mayhem such a contest would cause?

Thus the telephone choke system came into being. The phone company came up with a way to choke off calls made to WABC when the capacity threatened to overload a circuit. After a certain number of calls got regular busy signals, other callers would get a "busy circuit" signal. Lots of stations would have killed for such problems.

Trying to have a contest that would generate response but hold down the threat to the city's safety, the Truck-a-Luck chugged out of Rick's promotion machine. The brightly decorated WABC truck would be driven all over the listening area. Jocks would announce where the truck was going to be and how many people would get instant prizes.

"The first ten people to spot the Truck-a-Luck on the Grand Concourse in the Bronx will win big!" Ron Lundy (now holding down the 10 to 3 slot on WABC, since the network had finally understood that the WABC listener had no appetite for *The Breakfast Club* and Charlie Greer was in the nighttime shift) would shout.

Throngs would hurry to the Grand Concourse, presumably in an orderly fashion. The lucky people would win dinners or movie tickets, but occasionally the note inside the instant-prize envelope would tell the listener he'd won a color TV or a trip for two to Florida. The driver of the truck would take the listener to a pay phone to be put on the air live to tell the whole listening audience how thrilled he or she was. We'd take their reactions and assemble a promo spot that went something like this:

"EEEEEEEEEEK!" "Well, what do you know?" "You're

kidding!" "Yaaaaaaaaaaaay!" "I don't believe it!" "You're not kidding? EEEEEEEEEEK!"

"These lucky listeners spotted the WABC Truck-a-Luck and won big! Listen for the location of the Truck-a-Luck and you could win too!"

The Truck-a-Luck was more evidence that we weren't an untouchable, impersonal station. We were right there in the neighborhoods.

We had a magic formula, it seemed, and by 1968 one out of every four radio listeners was movin' and a-groovin', havin' a ball with Cousin Brucie. In radio terms that's called a 25 share. Today, New York radio stations routinely battle to see which station can garner first place with a 6 share.

It seems unbelievable that one station could command the audience that WABC did—impossible to imagine the power of an entity that had captured one fourth of the radio market in the biggest radio marketplace in America. But then those were impossibly unbelievable radio times, thanks, in large part, to the most powerful force in the history of recording, more powerful than rock 'n' roll itself. It was a force as compelling as it had been unanticipated and as unpredictable as it was eventually pervasive. It was four menchildren leading the young, beguiling the young at heart, and dancing beyond the control of the old. It was a moment in the history of the world called Beatlemania.

CHAPTER ELEVEN

Beatlemania

The 1964 Mustang was a power trip if ever there was one. Step on the accelerator of that baby and you'd fly. Bucket seats scooped into the interior of the car gave the driver a racing-car perspective on the world—perfect for a cocky, get-out-of-my-way attitude. There was a backseat, sure, but this automobile was meant to be a private, personal kind of experience. Unlike the sociable Chevies of days gone by, the Mustang was a declaration of independence, not a gathering place. America's peacetime factories were busy crafting tailor-made toys for the postwar babies. At the Ford Motor Company, a man named Iacocca had noticed that this segment of the United States' society was accustomed to having products made and marketed to it specifically, so he had wisely gone about designing a set of wheels that would be theirs alone. He and his engineers had come up with the Mustang—a wild stallion. The Mustang was a car that was the perfect chariot for the captain of the high school football team, a Cinderella carriage for the long-legged co-ed whose straight honey-blond hair blew so beautifully when the top was down, the appropriate pause for a newly graduated attorney, poised before upward mobility carried him to the sure Mercedes of his future.

Sonny and Cher drove matching Mustangs. Nothing more need be said, except that the Mustang was a way to go full speed ahead into the New Frontier we didn't yet realize had closed less than a year before.

In 1964, America had all the hysterical pseudogaiety of an Irish wake. Mourning for our fallen president, we eulogized and televised and synthesized the Kennedys in every way possible.

Mostly, though, we escaped.

We escaped with James Bond in films and with *The Beverly Hillbillies* on TV. On the one hand, we were fans of British sophistication and the wizardry of spy technology. On the other, we loved our strike-it-rich homeland where hicks could hobnob with bank presidents. Nowhere was our ambivalence about our time and place more apparent than in the blacker-than-black humor of a film about the misfiring of the H-bomb. *Dr. Strangelove or: How I Learned to Stop Worrying and Love the Bomb* confirmed our worst fears about the modern military while it mocked our lingering faith in good old American courage. A nation that had cut its teeth on *Sands of Iwo Jima* and the best of Audie Murphy was now fascinated by a portrayal of a hapless Pentagon and an eerie mad scientist who could not stop the involuntary "heil Hitler" salute bred into his right arm. In the midst of this festival of futurism, when the bomb was about to blow, we had a throwback. Slim Pickens, the consummate cowboy sidekick, rode that buckin' bomb, waving his Stetson like the rowdy but lovable rodeo riders who were so supremely American. Just like the buckaroo we had in the White House.

Yes, gone was the grace of the hatless Bostonians. A ten-gallon cowpoke who called us his "fellow 'murcans" was running the show now. He sped around his ranch in a grotesque gas guzzler. He had the jowlly look of a basset

146

hound, the paunch of everybody's Uncle Ed, and the foresight of Mr. Magoo. Talk about throwbacks. Our unelected president had come straight out of the classic smoke-filled rooms where political futures were decided by land deals sealed with bourbon and branch water. New England's cigar-and-brandy drawing rooms had hardly been the scenes of more idealistic transactions, but in three years we'd become used to thinking we were a country growing in elegance. We were almost two hundred years old, after all; it was time for a little poise—not the blue-blood manners of the Roosevelt old money, or the rigid military bearing of Ike, either. No, we'd grown happy with being the kind of country where the sons of sons of immigrants knew how to wear tuxedos and how to handle six or seven dinner implements as easily as a football.

Still, the rocking chair had been carried out of the White House, so the rock 'n' roll generation was on its own, disenfranchised from the country's leadership, disenchanted with the country as a whole. It's no wonder that salvation came from another country. In February of the year 1964, a force that even wild stallions couldn't keep pace with hit our shores. It was as unexpected as it was without precedent.

In early 1963, six or so "all-Americans" had sat in a music meeting at WABC and listened to a test pressing of a song called "I Want to Hold Your Hand." The British group who had recorded it were making it big in England and Germany, we were told. Word had it that they were going to make a pass at the U.S. market. "No way," one of us said. "Forget it." "Thumbs down." "Stupid name for a rock group." Sometime in 1964, the station was calling itself W-A-Beatle-C.

The Beatles first came to America on February 7, 1964. The very first of their three appearances on *The Ed Sullivan Show* gathered the largest television audience ever to watch any entertainment program. Still, Sid Bernstein, a concert promoter everybody at WABC knew, a nice, soft-spoken guy who absolutely believed every act he handled was the blockbuster of all time, booked them into Carnegie Hall, fearing even 2,700 seats might be too many to try to fill. So it began, both big and small, so great the crowds hoping to get a glimpse of them at a window of the Plaza Hotel were at times terrifying, so simple that when they went to Miami, the four boys frolicked in the surf and picked up stunned and silly sunbathers. Playful, they were called, and so we all played with the phenomenon—radio writing the rules as it went along.

Come with me to August 1964:

"So, cousins, the Beatles have their fifth number-one song of 1964. Tell you what . . . while I play 'A Hard Day's Night' you call and tell me who's your favorite Beatle. John? Paul? He's dreamy, huh girls? George—the shy one? Ringo . . . sweet, serious Ringo? Which one? Give me a call at WABC."

As always, the majority of callers are in love with Paul. I've been partial to John since the day I met the four ragamuffins when Sid booked them into Carnegie Hall. They were all likable, but still, I didn't feel any warmth for McCartney; he was so obviously insecure that all you got from him was a mask. John was clearly the leader, the most forthright. He seemed to be the most intelligent too; his humor was from the brain, while the others seemed to settle for clowning. George did seem shy, willing to let the others mug in front of the mike, and Ringo was more of a fan than the object of fans' interest. He loved New York, he wanted to be a New York disc jockey, he said. Beatledom was something that didn't seem to be real to Ringo.

I decide to put a girl who wants to vote for John on the air:

"OK, that was 'A Hard Day's Night,' by the Beatles. Who have I got on the line here?"

"Carol."

"What's your last name, Carol?"

"Rosenfeld."

"From?"

"The Bronx."

"Ah, the Bronx . . . do you know the special cheer?"

(GIGGLE)

"OK, Carol, tell the cousins who your favorite Beatle is."

"John."

"Tell us why."

"He's cute and he's talented and, I don't know . . . he's funny."
She spoke in a British accent. It happened every time a kid got on the
air to talk about the Beatles. They were going headlong into this British
thing.

"Well, Carol, that's terrific . . . and I'll tell you what. I've got four
tickets for you and your friends to see the movie 'A Hard Day's
Night'."

(SHRIEK!) "Oh, thank you, Cousin Brucie. Thank you."

"What's your favorite radio station, Carol?"

"W-A-Beatle-C!"

I've seen these geographic fads before. Rockabilly from the South, the
street-corner sounds of Philly, R&B from Motown, and surfers from
California. This British thing is just another local sound. It'll all blow
over once the newness wears off. In fact, last week "Rag Doll" was
number one. You can't get more American than four kids from
Newark. And look what's coming up on the charts: "Everybody Loves
Somebody," by Dean Martin. The more things change the more they
stay the same, I guess. Remember the Singing Nun in January? The
Beatles could turn out to be just another novelty act.

From the perspective of the eighties we see that they were
many things. They were the watershed, the Continental Di-
vide. The International Dateline. The absolute turning point in
rock 'n' roll. They were all of this and a hundred times this, but
they were no novelty act.

By August 1965 they were the biggest phenomenon the
recording industry had ever known. With merchandise from
change purses to hair spray to record players to the inevitable
Beatle wigs, they were an industry unto themselves. They were
separate in every way. Their music was no one else's. Their
enthusiasm was unlike anyone else's. They were able to tease,
yet be sweet. They were devilish without a hint of evil. They
had a perception of their place in entertainment and history
and a perspective on entertainment as history. Theirs was a

demeanor that was no one else's. The Beatles were conscious excellence with absolutely no self-consciousness.

The Battle of the Beatles was the fiercest war in the history of American radio. All over the country, stations bit, clawed, and scratched at each other, trying to be home of the mop tops. New York, home of the most, the biggest, the tallest, the strangest, the greatest, of course was the fiercest at the Beatles War. Murray the K, who'd met the Beatles on their first tour, declared himself "The Fifth Beatle" (a lapse of taste if not sense shared by many a jock in many a radio market). WABC taped the Beatles calling me from their limo saying, "Hi, Cousin Brucie. I'm John, I'm Paul, I'm George, I'm Ringo, and we love Cousin Brucie and WABC!" WMCA demanded acknowledgment as the "official" Beatles station. The brass ring on the Beatles merry-go-round was exclusive access to a new release. When a precious exclusive gem fell into our hands, the procedure for its debut was as intricate as the D-Day invasion, the handling of the recording done as gingerly as moving nitro. We'd spend thirty-six or so hours before the recording actually reached the studios promoting its upcoming, exclusive debut on WABC, entreating the listeners to stay tuned to the one station where they could hear more Beatles and could hear them *first*. If the song was to be played first in my show, the jocks would spend the whole day working the listeners into a frenzy. I'd go on and promise that this was the show they'd been waiting for . . . the moment was almost here . . . tonight I was going to play the latest Beatles release. Finally, finally, about halfway through the show, with every Beatlemaniac in thirty states blind with anticipation, the song would go on. The intro would go something like this:

> "OK, cousins, this is the moment we've been waiting for. It's just arrived. It's here in the studio. It's hot, hot, hot! It's the new Beatles record and I'm about to play it for you, but first we've got some serious business to attend to. You know, W-A-Beatle-C is the

only station to have this record. We're proud that the Beatles wanted us to have it first, so until they decide it's time for other stations to get it, we're going to make sure nobody steals it from us. While the song plays, you're going to hear the 'WABC Exclusive' jingle a few times. That's our way of keeping this record *exclusively* for us and our W-A-Beatle-C listeners, but don't you worry, you're going to hear the Beatles beautifully—on this fabulous new release. And now, let's get to it. Here it is, the Beatles' new release: 'Love Me Do,' *exclusively* on W-A-Beatle-C!"

We'd cue the song up again immediately. "Love Me Do" would play once more without further introduction, but with continued interruption by the "WABC Exclusive" sounder playing over the record. No other station could tape the song off the air without our call letters. No other station would play it with our call letters. The exclusive was protected. After its first airing, the Beatles tune was played at least twice an hour.

Our sister stations in the ABC network began to feel some sibling rivalry over our good fortune with the Beatles. Since the Cousin Brucie show reached well over half of the American markets, other stations were instantly flooded with requests for the new Beatles record. Without the record, their nighttime shows lost listeners and Beatle credibility. Rick started getting heat. John Rook, program director of the ABC affiliate KQV in Pittsburgh, finally demanded to know just what kind of a family the ABC family was. How could the flagship station grab ratings away from his operation? Absolutely fair question. Of course Rick would try, whenever possible, to arrange for the affiliates to have the exclusive too. Unfortunately, what with the mails and one thing or another, it would usually arrive a day or two after we received ours. All's fair in the Beatles war.

The war raged hotter in New York because so much of the action was actually being played out on our turf. After the Beatles stayed at the Plaza, the stations got the picture on how difficult it was to get to them in their hotel, a level of difficulty constantly escalating in direct proportion to their popularity. When they stayed at the Warwick Hotel on their next visit, WABC went after field position the way Montgomery stalked Rommel: suite right above the Beatles' Warwick enclave; arrangements for exclusive interviews from the rooms of the fab four; wireless mikes brought in for the occasion so our access to every word, breath, sneeze, was free of the constraint of cables. We'd set up a remote studio at the Warwick, and were ready to pipe every magic moment to the studio for broadcast—not only to our listening audience, but to the hundreds of ABC affiliates around the land. If there was ever a moment that solidified the power of WABC and the passion of being a part of it, the day the Beatles came to the Warwick was it.

The crowd had begun to gather before the sun had even cleared the lowest East Side buildings. The Beatles' plane wouldn't even touch down at JFK until afternoon, but by noon the police estimated fifteen thousand squealing, yearning fans behind the flimsy barricades lining Fifty-fourth Street and Sixth Avenue, known as Avenue of the Americas, but definitely Boulevard of the Brits today. There was no official count on the number of transistor radios, but the indications were that there were plenty. Broadcasting "Beatle Bulletins" (which, given how little happens when one is waiting for a plane, amounted to giving the listeners a feel for the theater of the event rather than real information about the progress of the foursome to Fifty-fourth Street), WABC kept radio's most rapt audience tuned in. Each time the Warwick Hotel was mentioned, every time reference was made to the eager crowd awaiting the group, a swell of sound began in the street and reached us where we waited. In essence, we were conducting a chorus of uncontrollable anticipation.

Leaning out of the eighth-floor window of the room where we were encamped, with Rick Sklar hanging on to my belt and his hopes for the broadcast of the century, I would take the cue from Dan in the studio across the street and report:

"Well, here we are in the Warwick Hotel, Dan." (SCREECH!) "Actually, I'm outside of the hotel, doing this report by the seat of my pants. Below me I can see a bevy of very beautiful Beatles fans." (SCREAM!) "They're waiting for the Beatles, Dan. We all are. As we heard from our Kennedy Airport team, they'll be in their limousine soon—and on their way here. We're ready for 'em and just as soon as we see the car driving up Fifty-fourth Street" (EEEEEEEEK!) "we'll let you know. This is your Cousin Brucie at the W-A-Beatle-C headquarters at the Warwick Hotel." (Yaaaaaaay!) "Back to you in the studio, Dan."

Every scream, every yell let us know that the audience was not only wired, they were tuned in. There was no doubt about who was the official Beatles station on that day. And we took that status very seriously. Although we knew from our crew at Kennedy that they wouldn't arrive for at least forty-five minutes, we were drawn to the window by wails that sounded like the Beatles must have been near. Sure enough, a tan Bentley was pulling up and four mod mop tops were running out.

I got the cue from the engineer and started to say, "This is it," but it didn't feel like it. The way the guys ran, without any bounce, the way they hesitated, without any fear . . . even though the crowd was surging and the police were straining, this didn't feel like the arrival of the Beatles. And it wasn't. A group called the Teddy Boys was trying to grab some publicity. Before they were found out, the rapturous gathering had stumbled over each other, had trampled the barricades, had shaken some mounted police from their mounts. If this was merely preview, what would the actual performance be like?

"That wasn't the Beatles. I repeat. That wasn't the Beatles. Some impostors have just tried to pass themselves off as the Beatles. The police are trying to calm the crowd. They have the foursome and they're taking them into the hotel. Stay tuned to

153

W-A-Beatle-C and we will have the *actual* arrival of the *bona fide* Beatles the moment it happens."

When it finally did happen, it happened the wrong way, which turned out to be the right way. After the Teddy Boy stunt, we saw Fifty-fourth Street become progressively emptier until there was no traffic on it between Sixth and Fifth avenues. The police linked arms and prepared to dam the flood of fans. I hung out the window and watched, looking not toward Fifth Avenue, but to the Sixth Avenue corner of the hotel. Fifty-fourth Street ran from Sixth toward Fifth, eastbound. Naturally the limos would be coming that way. But nothing about the Beatles in New York was natural and, wisely, the city's finest had decided to sneak them around the corner going the wrong way on the one-way street. Though the moment of confusion was brief, the police had bought themselves time enough to get the world's biggest rock group in motion toward the hotel before the crowd got in motion toward them.

> "They're here . . . they're here. The Beatles have arrived. They almost fooled us, coming the wrong way down Fifty-fourth Street, but there's no way to keep the Beatles a secret."

I was broadcasting and experiencing at the same time. I recalled a scene in a radio play read long before. It described a bombing. It said from the aircraft the chaotic crowd and its streaming blood looked like a flower blossoming. It was a macabre thought for such a lighthearted moment, but the scene did look like a flower unfolding. The police on horseback were the tight center of the flower. As the brightly dressed youngsters pushed against the horses, the center spread, the color reached everywhere, the tiny foursome rushed like petals in a strong wind.

> "I see John, there's Paul, now Ringo, yes, George is running in too. The fans are getting to them, the

police are there, though . . . they're inside the hotel. Dan, the Beatles have arrived at the Warwick. They're inside the hotel and we're on our way down to their suite. We'll get back to you the minute we see them. Back to you, Dan."

We had our mo-joe working. Rick had authorized persuasion of every security officer and hotel employee anywhere near the Beatles. WABC was enough of a force in the city that helping us get to the Beatles was not unlike helping the post office get the mail through. Soon enough we were in the suite, and as good as it was to have the actual Beatles to put on the air, we had a drama that was even better.

"Something terrible has happened, that I'm quite ashamed of—I know Scottso is too. Somebody took a medallion, a St. Christopher's medallion, right off Ringo's neck in the excitement, and I'm sure they didn't mean to do this. . . . Here's Ringo . . . Ringo?"

Ringo: "Hello, how are you . . . good to be back in New York anyway."

Me: "I'm sorry. Your shirt's been ripped. I don't like the way you look."

Ringo: "The only thing, the medallion, you know, I haven't had it off me neck since I was twenty-one. It's three years. It's sort of a keepsake, it's from me auntie . . . and . . . if anyone's got it . . ."

Me: "Can you describe it?"

Ringo: "It's just a gold St. Christopher . . . if anyone . . . "

Me: "It *is* gold?"

Ringo: "It *is* gold. . . . I only wear gold," he said, rolling his eyes.

Me: "Listeners, I tell you what you do—Ringo, we have a suite of rooms here. WABC has a suite of rooms right above you—now it is a gold medallion and it is very dear to Ringo. I know you want a souvenir, but if you bring it up to us, we'll see that you're rewarded."

Scott Muni: "As a matter of fact, I'm sure we can make this deal right now, with Ringo. Anyone who has the St. Christopher medallion that they tore off Ringo as he was coming in the hotel room, if you will come to our WABC suite, with the medallion, we will see that you meet Ringo *in person*. And he will thank you personally. If you will bring the medallion back. Now . . . Cousin Brucie and I are going to go down on the street now, because we know a lot of the people are listening to WABC right now down on the street and if you have the medallion, if you give it to us, we'll see that you meet Ringo personally, right?"

Ringo: "That's a deal."

It was a story somewhat smaller than what we'd made of it, but it kept the listeners tuned in as we pleaded for someone to come forward if they had the medallion. The media was picking it up. TV news was asking for information about Ringo Starr's medallion too. The phone call from Angie McGowan's mother came shortly after I went on the air that night. Her daughter had come home with the St. Christopher's medal and told her the story and that whoever had the medal was supposed to call Cousin Brucie. Was her daughter in trouble? Would the police need to be notified? In trouble? Angie would be a heroine! WABC would love to have her and her mother as our guests in the city that night, I said. We'd had a game plan worked out in case we heard from the "finder" of Ringo's medallion, and we had a room reserved across the street at the Hilton where we would hide the young lady and her mother until we could milk the drama some more. We graciously offered Mrs. McGowan and Angie our protection. When we determined listenership would be the highest, and fan and media appreciation of our inside track to the Beatles would be the greatest, and awe of our ability to make a young woman's dreams come true would be the finest, we would put Angie on the air. It happened on the Cousin Brucie show the next night. About a dozen reporters were there. Ringo had been smuggled across the street and was smiling shyly. Angie was there with her mother and four girlfriends (we weren't about to refuse her anything; we wanted this moment on the air).

"When we heard the police siren and saw the black limousine, I ran to the car. The car stopped and I came to the door and tried to open it, but I couldn't. I went around to the other side of the car and I saw John and then Paul was next and I went and touched his head, because I wanted to touch his hair. And then I saw Ringo—I wanted to kiss him more than any of the others, so I tried to get my arms around his neck to kiss him and when the whole thing was over I had the medallion in my hand."

So spoke Angie McGowan, as flashbulbs flashed and the nation listened. The ABC affiliates were getting this moment live, just as they'd taken the "feed" of the Beatles' arrival. Ringo kissed her and each of her friends. I broadcast the blow-by-blow of each buss and the drama came to an end.

For me, though, the drama was just beginning. I was going to be the one to introduce the Beatles to fifty-five thousand fans in Shea Stadium.

"Bruski," Sid Bernstein had said, "would you like to host the Shea Stadium concert? One thing: Would you mind if Ed Sullivan kind of co-hosts?"

To a concert and record promoter in the sixties, radio was the power. You asked the radio jock if the TV guy could come along. Ed Sullivan could come along, sure. The papers were predicting the apocalypse in Flushing Meadow. I wanted to be the one to host that concert, but I was more afraid than I'd ever been of anything. Anybody who wanted to stand on that stage with me was more than welcome.

Shea Stadium had been built as part of New York City's

World's Fair fanaticism. A baseball team called the Mets had been created three years before. Casey Stengel, a pride of the Yankees, was their manager. Given the colorful Casey, the hapless Mets, and the daffy sports fans who couldn't believe the Yankees were no longer the only game in town, Shea was more of a theater than a stadium. That theater was going to be tested to its greatest extreme at 8 P.M. on Sunday, August 15, 1965. And what of the disc jockey? What kind of test would he face on that night?

By 1965 I'd done a few appearances in prisons. At first I was terrified when the door clanked inexorably closed and was locked and double-locked into a barricade from which there was no escape. Still, I'd gradually become used to the sound and secure in my ability to leave when I wanted to. My learned comfort inside prison walls in no way prepared me for what I saw inside Shea that night. I had a physical reaction to the walls of fences and the barbed wire that topped them. In parts of the stadium, there were two layers of fence, both capped by jagged metal. Like the scenes in World War II films, there were guards patrolling the borders of the protected territory. Policemen walked in pairs, cautioning the crowd, mostly teenaged girls, mostly wearing cotton dresses, to keep back, take their seats, settle down. A tightness in my stomach threatened to make its way to my throat, but still there was a singing in my nerve endings, a rush at the risk of this. Radio jockeying is excitement in the safe world. This night was going to be exhilarating by anyone's definition of excitement.

For the time, the stage that was constructed just behind where second base should have been was monolithic beyond belief. Scaffolding enough to construct a skyscraper was supporting speakers that seemed to tower higher than anything visible on the skyline. A black wall from which the sound of the future would soon be rushing, this is what those fans looked to with more expectation, more sexual sensation than had ever been contained in any public place before.

I went to the backstage area that was actually under the

stage. Legitimate concert employees rushed past hangers-on. Anyone with any connection to anybody with any pull had tried to get into Shea that night. Press, corporate types, broadcast and record industry honchos, all hovered and tried to look as though they had a pipeline to four urchins who, by God, had grabbed the world by the balls and was making it scream for more. Sid was pale with terror. He slid in and out of what was obviously the Beatles' dressing room, ghostly in his tasks, uncertain of the moment. He waved me in.

"Amazing. Absolutely amazing," he said as we walked through a series of rooms. They're in here. I think they're scared."

" 'lo," said George.

" "lo, Cousin Bruce," said Ringo.

"Hey man, how's it goin'?" said Paul.

"Quite something, eh?" said John.

Subdued for the first time ever, the Beatles sat, feet up, smoking, staring, waiting.

"Good luck tonight, guys. See you out there." Equally subdued, I retreated.

"Good luck to *you*," came the farewell.

Sid finally came out of the dressing room at about 8:30 and said, "Let's get this thing going."

Somewhere before I got to the steps of the stage, I was joined by Ed Sullivan. Ed might as well have been attending a hanging—his own. The man who strode and stretched and grimaced in front of millions of Americans every Sunday night was turning to mush on this Sunday. He literally shook so badly that he leaned against me as we climbed the stairs. My dad had been with me at so many appearances by this time that the contact with the older man made me calm. On this night, one unlike any that had gone before or any that would ever come again in my career, I called upon the familiar ritual of son and father, protecting, protector, to steady myself.

Once the crowd saw us, all hell broke loose. If somebody, anybody, was up on that stage, could the Beatles be far behind?

"Please . . . please . . ." I pleaded into the mike. "Ladies and gentlemen . . . ladies and gentlemen . . ." I tried to quiet the bellowing beast. "This is your Cousin Brucie."

"Yaaaaaaaaaaaaay!" (Cousin Brucie meant rock 'n' roll and rock 'n' roll meant the Beatles.)

"The Beatles are here. They'll be with us in a moment . . ."

More roars, more screams . . . "Ladies and gentlemen, Ed Sullivan!"

Roaring, screaming, screeching. They knew Ed. He was the guy who pointed to center stage before the Beatles came on the TV screen.

"Helloo," he said. And then he looked at me. Ed Sullivan had nothing more to say to that crowd. Seven hundred people in a CBS studio were one thing. Fifty-five thousand fanatics in a baseball stadium were something else. If these boys make it through this, it will be a miracle, I thought. But it was a night to believe in miracles and so I said it sweet and simple.

"Ladies and gentlemen . . . the Beatles!"

A flying wedge of guards ran up the stairs, surrounding three guys with guitars and one with drumsticks. The cordon parted and there were the by-now-legendary Beatles. They looked so young. So small. They shook their heads, they moved their mouths. I was two feet away from a speaker the size of a pickup truck. All I could hear was the crying of the crowd. All anyone heard on August 15, 1965, was screaming. Though they'd toured four continents, the Beatles hadn't been heard in concert since 1963. Fans heard only the sound of themselves.

I walked down the stairs to view the stage from the field. I wanted to see the Beatles in concert too. A policeman approached and said, "Do us a favor, Cousin Brucie? Walk around with us. We've got to keep these girls calm."

And so I walked the borders of Shea that night. I talked to the girls who were crying. I talked down the ones who were climbing the fences. I watched them drop in dead faints. Sid had said the insurance and medical crews for the concert had cost a fortune. He was getting his money's worth. As fast as they went down, the white-suited medical teams got to them, put them on stretchers, and carried them away, the empty spot at the fence filled quickly by the mass of hysteria.

"She's missing the concert," I thought the first time a girl was carried off. Then, as it happened over and over, I realized that wasn't true. For some, passing out would be their memory of the Beatles at Shea, a battle wound as precious as any that ever earned a soldier a purple heart.

I didn't see the end of the concert. A policeman intercepted me and said, "Time to go. Your car's here." The security procedures had been elaborately choreographed. Getaway cars were scheduled as carefully as every detail of the concert had been. I leapt into a limo that was barely stopped at center field. We took off. I left the Beatles on stage that night, never looking back at the future that was standing there.

That was the last time I ever saw them together. John was the one whose path crossed mine most over the years to come, a blessing considering the affinity I'd felt from the very beginning. Once at a benefit in Central Park's Sheep Meadow, he looked at the gathering of at least a hundred thousand, drawn by his advertised presence, and cautioned, "I'm only going to talk. Do they know I'm not going to sing?"

"They know," I said. "They just want to be where you are."

He shook his head, still mystified by idolization, by people viewing people as anything but simply people.

The next time I was in front of a crowd in Sheep Meadow was long after my WABC days. Once again it was John Lennon who brought the people there. Tragically, it was in death that he gathered them, and I was barely able to believe I was broadcasting a vigil for the most vital Beatle of them all.

The shooting had happened while I was taking a long weekend in a secluded inn in Connecticut. At eight in the morning the telephone woke me.

"Bruce, will you go on the air with me? I'm doing a thing on Lennon's death."

It was Dan, assuming I'd heard the news the night before. My shock shocked him.

"Holy shit, you didn't know?"

No, I didn't know. And now that I did, I didn't believe it. Could Dan and I really be talking about the death of John Lennon? We'd voted thumbs down on that first Beatles test pressing in 1963, sitting in a room together. We'd out-Beatled every other radio station in New York City together. We'd kept America informed of every inch of the Beatles' progress into a hotel, and every minute of every stay they'd ever had in New York. The Beatles were the best of our shared experiences at WABC and now Dan and I were having the worst shared experience imaginable. The Beatles had been murdered.

The telephone rang several times after Dan and I said a quiet good-bye. Reporters wanted reactions, radio stations called for interviews. The program director of the station I now owned called for direction. Should we stick with the format? Should we go all Beatles?

Stick with the format. Let's not cash in on it. Let it be.

CHAPTER TWELVE

The Inside Story

So, with the help of the Beatles, the ratings showed that one fifth of all the nighttime radio listeners were listening to WABC. *The Cousin Brucie Saturday Night Party* was regularly capturing 25 percent—one out of four—of all the radio listeners in the New York City radio market. The other three went to the twenty-six other stations in the listening area. As glorious as things were, the ratings created pressure. Even though all logic and industry experience said a 25 share was impossible, there was pressure to stay there. If something isn't broken don't fix it. If only somebody could have carved that above the doors to the WABC studios. Soon, the station that had happened spontaneously, the sun that had shown with the brilliance of predictable unpredictability, was being poked and prodded and analyzed like some captured Starman being dissected to determine his powers. Soon, people were trying to "manage" the unimaginably lucky 77. Rick Sklar had been promoted to program manager in the fall of 1963 and it was under Rick's diligent and dedicated direction that the station rose to the amazing status it achieved. Still, even Rick couldn't resist the temptation to do the unspeakable—manage. The problem was we were unmanageable. Charlie Greer now had the slot after mine. Bob Dayton had Charlie's daytime shift. Anderson to Dayton to Ingram to Muni to Morrow to Greer. It wasn't exactly a roster of IBM robots. We were independent types; we functioned independently of any concern about station management. We were equally independent of one another, comrades on the air, oblivious to each other off. None of us ever saw each other "socially," with the exception of industry functions that masqueraded as social get-togethers.

Unable to have much control over such a staff, Sklar was going to manage the music—"scientifically." The playlist is the vocabulary of a radio station. If a song doesn't make the playlist, its title isn't spoken on the air. With the power of WABC at such mammoth proportions, our playlist was pretty much the make-it-or-break-it decision on all popular music. Rick Sklar was an absolutely honorable man. A record had to earn its way onto the WABC playlist, not by the old-time payola methods, but by having it in the grooves. Having it in the grooves meant that the popularity of the recording artist and the sound was undeniable. It was hard to miss with a Beach Boys or Elvis tune, for instance. A record could also have it in the grooves by having that elusive, but actual unmistakable mark of a hit, no matter how uninitiated the performer. In 1963, "It's My Party," by the then-unknown Lesley Gore, had that mark.

At WABC the heart of the selection process was the music meeting. In the old days, music meetings were elitist affairs, clubby get-togethers where the air staff, program manager, and assistant program manager (usually an all-male gathering) would sit around, scratch themselves, make crude remarks, and occasionally get serious about the record industry. It could be boring, but there was a certain feeling of power that went along with giving the yay or nay to a song, and we all went to the meetings rather than relinquish that power.

Rick thought things ought to be a bit more statistically accurate. In addition to his system of calling a random sample of the thousands of record stores in New York, New Jersey, and Connecticut, he wanted to monitor the tastes of our listeners by having a cross-section of society represented at the music meetings. Suddenly sales reps and secretaries appeared at the sacred gatherings. Many of these people were perfectly lovely and wonderfully articulate, but it didn't sit well with the lofty deejays to have such neophytes deciding the very fate of rock with their uneducated opinions. Did this forebode a spirit of populism that would threaten the godlike reign of the jocks?

Scott Muni apparently thought so. The increasingly tighter playlists that were coming out of the suspect meetings were a sore spot with him. As Rick Sklar tells it, Scott became increasingly more vocal about his unhappiness, and a part of his demise came over something as innocent as Louis Armstrong's recording of "Hello, Dolly."

The WABC formula was to play the number-one song once every sixty minutes. Hour after hour, day after day, week after week, Satchmo told Dolly she was "lookin' swell"—not exactly a snappy rock lyric. It seemed as if the song's chorus was prophetic: "Dolly, you'll never go away." Finally Scott had enough. He told Sklar he wanted the record off of his show. There was no way Rick was going to stray from his strict music format, so the two men reached an impasse. Dolly was the last straw for Scott Muni and he and the station soon reached a mutual decision that he would leave.

About two weeks before Scott left, Rick had called me into his office and showed me a manila folder with my name on the tab. It had a star on it.

"See this? This is yours," he said. "Be patient. Wait."

What the hell did that mean? I wondered. Running the programming of WABC was a heady position and I frankly thought it had gone to Sklar's head. I forgot about the conversation soon after it happened. When Scott left, I was given his shift. The 7 to 11 P.M. time slot was the plum of the business in those AM-dominated days. Years had passed since my debut on WINS. At 10 P.M. on WABC I had achieved all the success and recognition I'd ever dreamed of. Still, when I got the 7 to 11 teen shift, I got the brass ring. It felt like such sweet justice to once again have the shift that Murray took away from me. I was far from meek, but I felt as though I'd inherited the earth. So this was what the Sklar star had meant.

Though it isn't unusual for disc jockeys to jockey for positions, I hadn't angled to get Muni's slot. I truly had been happy in the late-night slot. In retrospect, though, it seems as if everything important in my career happened after that move. It isn't surprising that Scott's many loyal friends would rally around him. Connie Francis, for instance, didn't speak to me for years after Sklar shifted me to the spot that had belonged to her close friend. She didn't want to hear that Mr. Muni's stubbornness had been his undoing and that his departure from WABC had been a bilateral move.

In fact, Scott wasn't really up against an ultimatum. One could get around the Sklar system with a little ingenuity. I gradually learned the survival tactics from that master of mischief, the man whose shift mine now followed, Dan Ingram. Dan took programming edicts as a challenge to his creativity. Now that I followed him on the air, I got to observe firsthand the workings of his deliciously devious mind.

Dan came to work one day and found a primitive system of clocks, lights, and alarms rigged up in the studio. Sklar had just come back from one of his "fact-finding" missions and apparently had observed such a system in one of our sister stations. The idea was that whenever clock number one tripped a red light, the jocks were to play the number-one song. Clock number two and the blue light were the cues for the number-two song, and so on. When I got to the studio that evening I found a memo detailing this Pavlovian exercise. "What are we—apes?!" I screamed.

"Relax, man. There's an easy way to deal with this," Dan replied.

He showed me how to turn the clocks back so the lights never went on. Sklar understood that the protest could turn into a mutinous situation and the clocks soon disappeared.

Those clocks and lights had inspired us, though. Having tested our ability to circumvent them and what they represented, we had established a revolutionary spirit that we could call upon whenever management threatened to take things too seriously. In about 1968, when Rick dictated that WABC would play no pre-Beatles tunes, it was time for the Resistance to surface once again. We gradually relabeled almost every oldie in the WABC collection. "Earth Angel" suddenly was dated 1968; "In the Still of the Night" had debuted in 1967, according to our system. To keep things honest we left some dates unchanged. "Greenfields" by the Brothers Four remained a 1960 tune. Lawrence Welk's "Calcutta" never strayed from 1961. Still, there was no way the radio rock giant could do without "Runaround Sue," "Duke of Earl," or "Are You Lonesome Tonight?" so they and others became more recent hits, according to the Ingram/Morrow system of chronology.

Again the message was received and things went on as they had before.

We once made our point about ridiculous systems and procedures at the expense of a radio rookie named Jay Reynolds. He'd been hired to take the overnight shift and he was just learning the ropes when he came to the studio one night to find two candles burning. All the jocks had received the candles as part of a promotion for a TV broadcast of the film *Bell, Book and Candle*. All except the new guy Jay, that is. Instead, he received a detailed memo telling him that since the station was studying various methods of energy conservation, these candles had to be closely monitored. He was to measure the candles every half hour and to call Rick Sklar at home the instant one of them went out.

An earnest overnight deejay who hopes someday to have a better shift tries to impress the program manager. Young Jay's eyes never strayed from those candles that night and sometime between four and five in the morning the first candle extinguished itself. He hurried to dial Rick's number. Our erstwhile program manager answered groggily.

"A candle went out," he heard.

"What?"

"One of the candles just went out," Jay explained. They sorted things out after Jay read Rick the memo. The author or authors of that prank were never discovered.

Whenever Rick came back from visiting other stations, it seemed he brought back yet another scheme for even greater success. He would get all kinds of inspirations while he was on the road. The clocks and lights had appeared after a road trip. New jingles arrived on his return from another odyssey. Ideas for "streamlining procedures" or "tightening the sound" followed him back from those forays away from the station, the inevitable products of his having had time to think about managing rather than continue with his trustworthy instincts.

Dan and I would joke about the crusty old New Yorker who ran the newsstand in the lobby of the WABC office building.

"He's the guy who's really running the station," we would say. "Rick goes downstairs and gets his ideas from that guy."

Mimicking, Dan would whine, "So, Maxie, what do you think of Mick Jagger? Mick Jagger, you know, the Rolling Stone. What's that, Maxie? He's a dirty little boy who should have his mouth washed out with soap? Right! I'm going upstairs to issue a No Rolling Stones memo right now!"

It was either memos about music or convoluted policies about how much talk between records or how many times the jingles were played per hour.

"Maxie's been after him," we'd declare knowingly. Truthfully, though, Rick was the chef mixing a stew of ideas, music, and information. Like all great chefs, he was open to the techniques that worked for others. Still, the trouble started when he began to doubt the public's taste for stew. He began to think about serving white bread—to second-guess why listeners were occasionally leaving our place to dine on the FM feasts.

Rick's radio restaurant had been built on the ingenuity and creative energy of the wacky cooks who had air shifts. When he started to force us to stick to the management's recipes, the spice went out of the food. Hand us a microphone and we swinging seven would do just about anything to get the listeners slightly looped.

We were looped ourselves. Inside the station, we had an atmosphere not unlike the one that would later be pictured in the film and TV show M*A*S*H: There was the nutty government coming across with policies that didn't have much to do with the front lines. Practical jokes were the only practical way of dealing with an insane success that was as fragile as our egos. The relabeling of the records, turning back the clocks, setting up the candles, were our intensely practical way of keeping control of a Camelot we were afraid would disappear.

The finest all-time practical joke was one that was sublime in its simplicity and one that God Himself wanted to happen. That's the only explanation of how I happened to be in the studio with precisely the right equipment when the right moment presented itself.

I hate to shop. Because of this I buy things in huge quantities whenever I get myself into a store. One afternoon I'd been shopping for underwear and had bought at least three dozen pairs of jockey briefs. The salesman had stuffed them into a large crinkly bag and I had headed to the studio. I walked in holding my bag of underwear during Dan's shift. He was doing the weather and he came to this line:

"There will be brief showers tonight."

I couldn't believe my good fortune—*brief showers!* I tossed the bag up in the air with all my might. It hit the ceiling, split open, and showered Dan with briefs. His eyes opened wide and he paused. After no more than a heartbeat, he collapsed in laughter. Every time he tried to speak he cracked up.

Kemosabes throughout the listening area were riveted to their radios. For twenty minutes the legendarily stoic Mr. Ingram could not get control of himself. He'd cue the engineer to play a song, regain his composure, and when the song had finished, lean into the open mike, only to lose it all over again. The brief showers episode—the one joke that broke up the unbreakable Ingram—ranks with the Beatles in Shea Stadium, the first time I broke into double-digit ratings, and the birth of my son as one of my proudest WABC memories.

Radio freaks all over the country have told me they have copies of that tape. I don't need a tape to replay it. It's indelibly etched on my mind as one of those moments when all of life's mysteries and miseries paused to allow for the healing powers of laughter.

Healing power was beginning to be called for as the station seemed to be changing into a business, and we would need even more as the world started to change around us.

CHAPTER THIRTEEN

The Handwriting on the Wall

Top 25 Songs of the Sixties

1. "The Theme from *A Summer Place*," Percy Faith
2. "Hey Jude," The Beatles
3. "Tossin' and Turnin' " Bobby Lewis
4. "I Heard It Through the Grapevine," Marvin Gaye
5. "I Want to Hold Your Hand," The Beatles
6. "I'm a Believer," The Monkees
7. "Aquarius/Let the Sunshine In," the Fifth Dimension
8. "Are You Lonesome Tonight?" Elvis Presley
9. "In the Year 2525," Zager and Evans
10. "It's Now or Never," Elvis Presley
11. "Love is Blue," Paul Mauriat
12. "I Can't Stop Loving You," Ray Charles
13. "To Sir with Love," Lulu
14. "Cathy's Clown," the Everly Brothers
15. "Big Girls Don't Cry," the Four Seasons
16. "Big Bad John," Jimmy Dean
17. "Sugar Shack," Jimmy Gilmer and the Fireballs
18. "Honey," Bobby Goldsboro

19. "People Got to Be Free," the Rascals
20. "Sherry," the Four Seasons
21. "The Ballad of the Green Berets," SSgt. Barry Sadler
22. "Get Back," the Beatles
23. "Can't Buy Me Love," the Beatles
24. "Sugar, Sugar," the Archies
25. "Ode to Billie Joe," Bobbie Gentry

Some truths about the music of the sixties, the Beatles, radio, and rock 'n' roll: *Billboard* (the source of all reliable music industry statistics, the Bible of radio and rock), in its charts of the top records by decade, reveals that the Beatles had four singles in the top twenty-five songs of the sixties. Two were released in 1964, the first year of America's Beatlemania. The other two were released at the end of the decade, in 1968 and 1969, practically the end of the group itself. Look at what was number one—"The Theme from *A Summer Place*"—a mainstream tearjerker if ever there was one.

Those four Beatles recordings are the only Beatles singles on the chart of the top one hundred songs from 1955 to 1984. "Hey Jude" is recorded as the twelfth most popular song of that era, and the most popular of all Beatles tunes. In fact, the group doesn't show up again on that chart until "I Want to Hold Your Hand" at number thirty. "Get Back" and "Can't Buy Me Love" are numbers eighty-nine and ninety respectively.

In *Billboard*'s Records of Longevity chart (the top forty records making the Top Forty for more than twenty-two weeks), the Beatles have zero.

Look back at the top twenty-five of the sixties. How much hard rock do you see? How much heavy metal? What's the ratio of protest songs to flag-waving songs? Look again. Not one Rolling Stones tune. In fact, looking at all the significant charts—Top 100 Records, Records of Longevity, Top Artists of the Sixties, Top Records of the Sixties—the Rolling Stones appear only once, as the twelfth most popular recording stars of the sixties, yet none of their recordings make any of the charts.

How can this be? Everybody's dominant impression of the sixties is the British invasion. Randy rock with questionable lyrics. Hard-hitting, get-down-and-boogie guitar riffs. Drugs. Psychedelia. Beatles, Beatles, Beatles, with a healthy measure of the Rolling Stones thrown in. How is it possible that the top twenty-five songs of the sixties include such memorable and enduring artists as Lulu, Jimmy Gilmer and the Fireballs, Zager and Evans, and Staff Sergeant Barry Sadler, not to mention the biggest nongroup of all time, the Archies—an animated amalgamation of recording-studio musicians brought together to create the sound of a cartoon show—but no Stones.

What the charts show is the handwriting on the wall. In the sixties, the charts reflected the music that was being played on AM radio stations and consequently bought by AM-radio listeners. So, though the charts show that soft rock and music not unlike that of the fifties was the most popular music, what anyone who was awake to what was happening in music in the second half of the sixties knows is that people were buying the Rolling Stones, and the Beatles did have popular songs other than their four on the top-25 charts. Groups like Blood Sweat and Tears and Crosby, Stills, Nash and Young were major forces in recording. Where were they? Not on singles charts, because they were recording albums and releasing songs from those albums. By the end of the sixties, 45 RPM records—the platters that had served up the hottest rock from about 1955 to 1965—were losing ground to 33⅓ LPs. Recording technology and recording artists were becoming more and more sophisticated. It wasn't practical or feasible to go into a studio simply to release a single. Where the singer and a studio band had once been recorded simultaneously, different components of a song were now being recorded onto different tracks and later "mixed" to yield the most dynamic sound. This procedure meant hours and hours of recording, mixing, and overlaying, hours that could only be cost-effective when invested in recording an album. And albums were recorded in stereo. Stereo, the six-letter four-letter word to AM radio.

By the end of the sixties, AM was hanging on to singles like a drowning man hanging on to a small lifesaver while the real lifeboat motors away to a party on the shore. The Top Forty records were no longer the pulse of the music industry. Baby boomers had stereo systems now. Record players and hi-fi sets looked like cheap toys compared to the tuners, amps, turntables, and speaker units that were finding their way into the homes and dormitories of America. People who were buying albums were getting attuned to the fullness, the richness, the availability, and yes, the reality, of stereophonic sound.

The switch was on and it was the most powerful switch in all of radio, and probably broadcast, history. The switch was from AM to FM and it heralded the death of Top Forty radio.

FM, for Frequency Modulation, had always been the repository of classical music and jazz—serious stuff of interest to only a handful. Since AM (Amplitude Modulation) had the listeners, AM had virtually all of the advertising dollars. Until the sixties, radios with the FM band were most likely the companions of reclusive radiophiles who probably also liked to monitor the short-wave band. Most important, FM listeners were insignificant in the eyes of the merchants of pimple creams, cigarettes, toothpaste, and soft drinks. Commuters, housewives, and above all, teens with transistor radios all but implanted in their ears were the people the sales staff was hawking. Hurry. Hurry. Hurry. Come one, come all. Put your message on WABC and reach nearly all of the disposable income in the tri-state area—and three dozen additional states at night. Many owners of both AM and FM stations treated the FM stations as stepchildren, programmed in hand-me-down simulcasts of their nurtured moneymaking AM operations.

Wally Schwartz himself, the farsighted genius of a general manager at WABC for four years, now says that in the early sixties no one could persuade him that FM was going to be a viable force in radio. The station signals drifted, the listeners were used to AM, there were so few radios equipped for FM, and why should there be? AM was serving people just fine.

Wally's assessment was the consensus. If visionaries like him were unprepared for FM, there simply was no way of predicting what happened.

FM's metamorphosis into a significant broadcasting force began in the mid-sixties, when the Federal Communications Commission ruled that owners of AM and FM stations could not use the same programming on each of them. Well, what the hell could you put on FM that wouldn't cost an arm and a leg and drain your AM operation? Hey, how about album cuts? Stations were getting free albums every day of the week. AM stations knew the wisdom of sticking to Top Forty singles, but maybe album cuts would work on the FM side since only serious, sophisticated, or spaced-out types listened to it. FM was different, and smart station managers capitalized on that difference. Rather than simulate the sound of the Top Forty format, they would stimulate the growing drug culture with the way-out music that went along with marijuana and recreational pharmaceuticals. The owners reasoned they could hire strange hippies as FM disc jockeys, letting them play whatever they thought their contemporaries wanted to hear, and, best of all, since they would be on "underground" FM stations, they wouldn't command big salaries like their AM counterparts.

FM jocks were a whole different breed. Lots of these guys were like the college kids who had to start their own fraternities because none of the mainstream frats would have them. They were definitely not your traditional AM-radio personalities. Still, they seemed to understand the strange sounds on some of the avant-garde albums that were becoming popular. Not the least bit intimidated by what Tom Wolfe would call the "Spam in a Can" jocks who had just hung on to the rock rocket and jabbered, the FM guys were cool—so cool they didn't have to shout. They spoke the language of the laid-back, no-hassle generation. These guys weren't crass pushers of products. No sir. Since the kind of advertisers who would be attracted to the FM kind of listener were more than likely space cadets from the Age of Aquarius too, their commercials were somehow less . . .

commercial. Waterbed stores, restaurants that specialized in bean sprouts, clubs that featured jug-band music, these were likely FM advertisers. These establishments didn't come with loud jingles or frenetic comedy spots. They wanted the comatose announcer to give a nice, near-whisper delivery to their soft-sell pitch. It went something like this:

> "Hey, if you happen to be out near that cool broken-down railroad station, maybe groovin' on the sunset or taking your old lady for a love-in, why don't you drop in to Mona's Magic Mushroom? Yes, Mona, the freak who sells granola shampoo door to door, has opened a place where vegetarians can eat in peace, love, and good health . . ."

The best FM announcers sounded like they'd been awakened from a deep sleep, as if they could barely concentrate long enough to read a spot before they nodded off again.

Where AM radio screamed about drag strips and twist lounges, FM told you in confidence that they knew where the party was, but keep it quiet, "we don't want the fuzz to find out, do we?" Where the most successful jocks on AM sounded like they'd love a piece of your bubble gum, the rising stars of FM sounded like they knew where you kept your stash of pot.

Deceptively indifferent in demeanor, the early FM air personality wielded great power, the power of being left alone to decide what would be heard on the air. It had taken station management about ten years to understand rock 'n' roll. They had no idea what to make of the more "artistic" sounds of esoteric album cuts. Better to let the long-hair jocks who talked as if they were walking through pudding play what the hippies and yippies wanted to hear.

Gradually, the Doors, Led Zeppelin, Jimi Hendrix, and Janis Joplin made their way on to radio. Six-minute cuts could easily be accommodated with the light FM commercial load. Since AM was where people got their news, weather, traffic reports,

Scenes from the exclusive
WABC live Beatles broadcasts

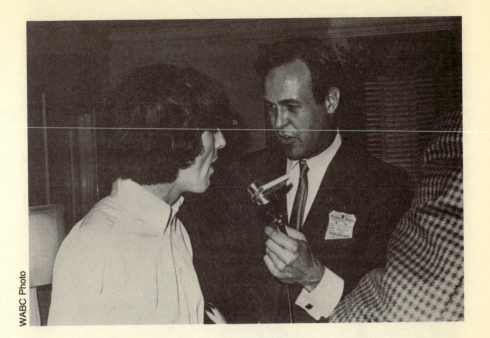

The definition of Beatlemania. Shea Stadium, August 1965.

Cousin Brucie in the comics

The Dave Clark Five looked like executives on the day they visited WABC.

Bat Bruce

Bobby Rydell and the Shangri-las on *The Go Go Show*

America's sweethearts, Joey Heatherton and Troy Donahue, on *Go Go*

Herman's Hermits were crowd pleasers on *The Go Go Show*.

An armful of love. Jon, nine, Meri, two, Paige, seven, in 1971.

Diana Ross and the Supremes worked through the night taping a *Mod Mod World* special.

Bill Mitchell—Paramus, N.J.

When Cousin Brucie got his
Saturday-night television show in
1972, he got old friends like Paul
Anka to add star power.

Private collection of Bruce Morrow

The fabulous Four Seasons, more glitter for the Saturday TV show

On the air on WABC

Eighty thousand fans came to hear John Lennon speak in Central Park in 1975.

John's good friend Harry Nilsson joined us onstage, and the fans went wild.

Cousin Bob Hope's TV special
from Central Park

Hello, Dolly.

Wagner International Photos Inc.

Hamming it up with Sha Na Na

Private collection of Bruce Morrow

Teaching Billie Jean my killer grip

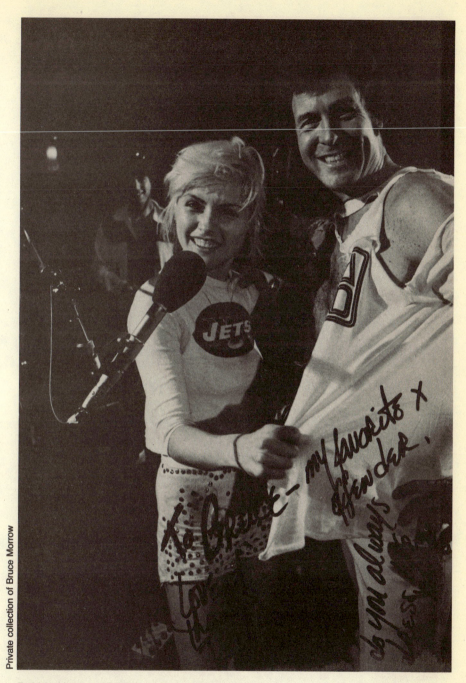

Debbie Harry couldn't keep her hands off me.

Let's go surfin'. (Left to right) Cousin Brucie, Beach Boys Mike Love and Al Jardine, Norm N. Nite.

Monty and Brucie making deals for Variety, the children's charity, on their annual telethon.

My hero, Mr. T., on the Variety telethon

Let's twist again, Chubby.

Jodie and Brucie doing what the Romans do while on vacation in Italy

and sports scores, there was virtually no need to take up FM air time with information. "MacArthur Park" was a seven-minute, twenty-second AM legend—a marathon-length aberration that became every jock's bathroom break in 1968. On FM, however, it was the norm to hear something like Dylan's "Like a Rolling Stone," a cut that ran six minutes and nine seconds. The young people who called themselves freaks liked this pacing. They liked that the guy on the air sounded like he was into baked bananas—liked that he wasn't peddling something every three and a half minutes. Finally, finances and supposed financial wisdom was the undermining of AM and the impetus for the final declaration of independence of FM. Many of the owners of the AM/FM combos found that the additional expense of staffing their FM stations, no matter how small, was a drain of AM revenue. FMs went up for sale at distress prices and gradually were sold to people with vision and without the constipation of conservative AM thought. These were people who understood that the clarity of the FM signal was better suited to the more mature, intricate stereo rock 'n' roll that was emerging, and who understood the power and potential of the music itself.

Early FM was an alternative to AM radio. Perhaps it wouldn't have so successfully supplanted AM and had such a dramatic impact on the country's radio listening preferences if America hadn't been so desperately seeking alternatives. By the middle of 1968, we were a country of shame, a country that had witnessed the assassination of the Kennedy brothers and Martin Luther King while standing by powerlessly. We were powerless to help them, to discover the truth about who wanted them dead and why, or to replace them with leaders equally strong and idealistic. Ideals, in fact, were going out of style among the establishment. It was clear that the baby boomers were going to have to develop alternative life-styles if they didn't want to give up their visions of an ideal society— visions that had been given to them by the hopeful postwar parents who were accustomed to seeing the government as always right.

The divisions—FM versus AM, idealism versus realism, offspring versus parents, progovernment versus antiestablishment, bubble-gum singles versus druggie albums—would perhaps have remained fragments, occasional quarrels, except for the most fateful, pivotal, unimaginable event in our nation's history. We were finding out about a tragic struggle that would polarize the United States of America as it hadn't been divided since the Civil War. We were hearing about a place called Vietnam.

In 1967 the platforms on which the divided country would stand were clearly defined. Suddenly music began to provide strong planks that would support the weight of an entire generation. *Rolling Stone* magazine published its first issue in 1967. In January 1967, people like Allen Ginsberg, Jerry Rubin, and Dr. Timothy Leary had joined with twenty thousand flower children for something called the Human Be-In. Staged in Golden Gate Park in San Francisco, the Be-In featured the music of the Grateful Dead and Jefferson Airplane, among others. These were not AM acts. This was the first big step in taking outdoor rock 'n' roll from the nation's intimate Palisades Parks to the acreage necessary for the rock festivals to come. Indeed, Monterey Pop, a three-day fifty-thousand-fan event, was to happen in June. This nearly religious rock raucous introduced Otis Redding and Ravi Shankar and drew on the talents of such luminaries as the Byrds, the Mamas and the Papas, Buffalo Springfield, and Laura Nyro. Significantly, it gave Janis Joplin, the Who, and Jimi Hendrix what was literally the first major arena in which to present their work.

Most important, though, was a day in early June when the one record album that would shift the course of rock forever had its debut. Its cover gathered the priests and rogues, the royalty and scoundrels of music, entertainment, and history. In front of this crowd stood four boys dressed in military costume. Mustachioed, and serious, the quartet were frozen in time behind a gaily painted drum reading SGT. PEPPER'S LONELY HEARTS CLUB BAND.

This was the moment when the past became prologue, when history and destiny became separate, with the conservatives hearkening to history and the radicals demanding to have a hand in destiny. With its songs both melodic and meaningful, this album pushed rock from the prosaic present to the explosive future. Time now points to *Sgt. Pepper* as the first concept LP. Musicologists say that with the appearance of this album, art rock came into being. Art and LPs. This is when the establishment barricaded themselves in AM radio and the freewheeling free thinkers swung wide the doors of the FM mentality. In fact, just as the Beatles were introducing their milestone album, a Los Angeles band that couldn't have been born without the Beatles was entering the pop charts in the dawn of its national recognition. The record was called "Light My Fire." The band was appropriately named the Doors. Yes, the doors to tomorrow were wide open.

By the end of 1967, *Billboard* reported that, for the first time in history, the record industry enjoyed one billion dollars in sales, noting that, also uniquely, album sales at 192 million outstripped the 187 million singles sold.

Indeed, 1967 was explosively pivotal.

In late 1967, the Beatles turned down Sid Bernstein's offer of one million dollars to once again play Shea Stadium. The boys had grown into something far bigger, far more powerful than a concert act in the two years since their first Shea concert.

It was in that same 1967 that Murray the K lost his job again. This time at WOR-FM. Bill Drake, a format fanatic and pro- gramming consultant, said that Murray had an "inability to live with direction." For the first time, Murray and I were in the same camp. I understood his rejection of strangling format rules—rules that were all the more constraining on AM sta- tions.

With FM largely identified as the freewheeling radio band, AM had become the radio of rigidity. Digging in against the FM enemy and fearful of the exodus away from Top Forty radio, management of the expensive AM monoliths began hiring consultants to develop "policies." At WABC, memos began to fill my mailbox. Though I didn't read them, reasoning that good news would reach me when I needed to know it and bad news would probably get there before I needed to hear it, I nevertheless felt the effect of whatever was inspiring those memos. Where staff meetings had once been brainstorming sessions, they were now occasions for handing down edicts. By 1968 I began to see what the sons of business—the "S.O.B.'s" who were tightening their grip on the AM band—were doing to what had been the most easygoing entertainment medium in history, but I still tried to close my eyes to it.

I'd been brought up with the government-as-guru training of second-generation Brooklyn. I'd been in the air-force reserve and gotten to wear a leopard-skin tuxedo on the days when I was supposed to be in uniform. I was pulling down a big salary from a huge broadcasting corporation with sponsors who were being boycotted by the long-haired tie-dyed fans of FM.

Where did I stand? Prowar or antiwar? Proformat or antitraditionalist AM? Pro–freedom of expression or antiprogress? Society was calling for people like me to commit themselves one way or the other, but it was still early for me. It was still the sixties. I believed the sensational, silly sixties would wash over all the seriousness that was in the air now. I was going to try to be aloof from the controversy. My mission was to entertain, not to take stands. I was convinced that though it seemed a bit nervous, WABC could be immune to politics and controversy. We were the phenomenon that defined the word *popular*. We were the captain of the football team, class clown, and most likely to succeed rolled into one. Everybody loved us. We didn't have to get involved in partisan squabbles.

Naturally, hindsight teaches us that there was no way to be immune from the festering that grew out of Vietnam. There was no hiding place. The truths that are now revealed by comparing the music charts of the sixties with the reality of the music of the sixties were political as well as musical truths. I was being tested again. For the first time in my life, I refused to admit it.

CHAPTER FOURTEEN

The Fading Flowers

In 1968 the sleek, in-a-hurry-to-get-to-the-top-of-the-corporate-ladder automobile was replaced by the practical, humble, rambling van. Inside the van were kids who called themselves freaks. I wasn't exactly in tune with these kids and they weren't exactly tuned in to AM radio. Rejecting the pursuit of money as a mark of materialism, the Be Here Now hippies became nomadic, no station's audience. They took off with only what was important to them—record albums, T-shirts, fringed vests, and bell-bottoms, along with a mattress, a guitar or recorder, an occasional dog, and half a dozen friends—and they hit the road.

From the distant outside of my position as a mainstream urban jock, the vans looked somewhat childish. It was almost as if the kids had taken the bright wallpaper of their toddler bedrooms and the illustrations of their first storybooks and processed them through fun-house mirrors. Amorphous blossoms floated around these flower children, and they floated too; they were rootless flowers. There was a naiveté in their wandering ways. Every experience was called a "trip." Like one of their early heroes, Holden Caulfield, they were running away from authority, and testing their wings. They were registering their protests against a society that would send its sons to war. Their protests were more vocal and outrageous than anything I'd seen from youth before. The word *fuck,* once unspeakable and unimaginable outside of locker rooms or in mixed company, seemed to be an all-purpose expletive. Young women talked about "balling" guys.

Aggressive and angry, the offspring of the peace-loving, prosperity-embracing products of the fifties tempered their crudeness with a "life is groovy" approach to most things. It was important to stay away from "hassles," lest one become "bummed out." Natural was better. Making your own sandals and jewelry was good. Embracing folklore and herbal cures was good. Hair that fell exactly as it grew, without the benefit of trim, style, or sometimes washing, was good. Back-to-the-earth farming was good. Above all else, banding together was good. Being with crowds of freaks sharing experiences, pot, and love was very, very important. Communal life was regarded as the purest way to live unselfishly. Because of this, the young grouped and regrouped regularly. People "crashed" for the night in other people's apartments and stayed for six weeks. When they heard about some groovy scene in Boston, San Francisco, or Boulder, they took off again. They were on the loose.

Thus, battalions of young people spread themselves across the nation. Rejecting commonplace jobs and concerns, burning their draft cards, they had little need for the information that propelled the Mr. Joneses of the country. Distrusting simplistic jargon and attitudes, they took as their own a kind of music with origins in far-off lands, drugs, or the simple folkways of America. This literal and figurative van-guard of the youth movement had no need for AM radio.

Yet, AM kept "those hits a-comin'."

Come with me to August 1968:

I walk to the studio as I always have, waving to the cruising cops, stopping for a succulent Sabrett hot dog with sauerkraut from my favorite vendor, jingling the coins in my pocket. The father of two with a wonderful apartment in Brooklyn and a summer place out on Long Island, I am where I always expected to be, doing what I've always dreamed of doing, yet noticing that the world around me does not seem as innocent as it once did. The kids I pass on the street ask for my spare change or stare through glazed eyes at whatever colorful sight penetrates their stupor and captures their attention.

In the studio, though, things are just about the way they've always been, thank God. I wave to Dan as I go to prepare my show and record the commercials and promos requiring my voice. Sometimes I stop in the studio and kibitz with Dan, but not since the brief-showers episode have I tried to break him up. Besides, these days aren't as lighthearted as the ones gone by. I'm impatient to get on the air.

Finally Cosell is speaking of sports. He's broadcasting from the studio today, an increasingly rare occurrence. He's got a phone hookup in the basement of his home and he prefers to broadcast from there. Aloof from the disc jocks as if sports jocks and the Mets are more socially relevant than the Beatles, he prides himself on his trenchant observations and is relentless in his self-promotion as one of the few true intellectuals in radio. Though WABC is a stew of many ingredients—not the bland oatmeal that the less successful, less sophisticated stations dish out— Howard's overrich speech and syrupy self-aggrandizement don't feel right with the spice of the air staff's sardonic ways. Frankly, he's boring, and nobody much cares that he's a member of the New York Bar. Radio seems more relevant than corporate legalese, these days. Music has gotten to be social commentary after all, and among the mavens of this music, Cosell is a bit of a schlemiel.

I could probably ease some of the stiffness of the Cosell situation if I would jaw with him about sports. But I know next to nothing about athletes or their world. In fact, I'm not sure whether it's time for the Super Bowl or the World Series and I couldn't care less. For me, like most radio people, the jock in disc jockey has nothing to do with athletics. I haven't participated in a team sport since the days of the sand-lot wars.

Finally it's my time to be where the world seems right to me. In the studio, on the uncomfortable swivel chair, shifting my weight, shuffling through the log, getting the kinks out. At 7:13 I'm waiting for the end of a news report about Richard Nixon's growing lead in the Gallup Poll. It looks as though clean Gene McCarthy, the poet senator, doesn't have a chance. It's clear that the benign Hubert Humphrey is going to be the sacrificial lamb in the November election.

Bobby Ryan (who amazingly is going to go on to be elected a state senator in Nevada despite the blindness that was just beginning when he was an engineer) hits the Cousin Brucie shouts ("Cousin Brucie . . . COUSIN BRUCIE . . . COUSIN BRUCIE!!!!) and then segues to the Frankie Valli jingle with the precision of a ballet dancer. Once again, for about the two thousand, one hundredth time, I greet the universe of WABC listeners.

"Yeeeeeeeeee! Hello, my cousins. Oh, what a beautiful night . . . summer vacation . . . you're free to be with your sweetheart on the beach tomorrow . . . and tomorrow night . . . mmmmmmmmm. In honor of summer freedom, let's start the show with the number-one song in the country, 'People Got to Be Free,' by my friend Sid Bernstein's phenomenal group . . . the Rascals!"

Russia is invading Czechoslovakia at this very moment, but rock 'n' roll knows better. We in the music world are arrogant enough to believe that if we play the song often enough we'll eventually get our message through to the Reds and they'll see the light of democracy.

There are plenty of precedents for believing that rock is a political medium. Just last month, Gram Parsons, the Byrds' singer/guitarist, refused to go on the band's tour of South Africa. He said he wouldn't play in a country where the segregation of blacks from whites— something called apartheid—was legal. This is interesting, considering that my own industry, an industry that the Byrds and all rock groups couldn't exist without, is far from color-blind. Few blacks are on the air on the top rock stations in the top markets. Black is a genre in radio, a separate sound. Thankfully, Rick Sklar understood that it didn't necessarily need to be and monitored the black stations for a guy that wasn't a victim of the stereotype. He found Chuck Leonard at WWRL in 1965, a guy who had self-confidence, poise, and a city-wide sound.

Chuck's been following me on the air ever since I've been in the 7 to 11 slot, and it's he whom I listen to at the end of my day, like the hundreds of thousands of listeners who keep his ratings as astronomical as they consistently are.

"Hello, I Love You," by the Doors, is still high on the charts. I don't particularly like that song, but it's a lot more mainstream than "Light My Fire" was. I'll have to play it after I slip in an oldie by the Supremes. I hear Diana Ross is going to split from the group. That'll give me something juicy to talk about. I'll probably open the phone lines and put the fans on the air. I can hear them already:

"Cousin Brucie. I can't believe Diana Ross would leave the Supremes. I mean they belong together, you know? I mean she's so beautiful and they all dress so boss and they're really good friends. I mean they went to high school together, right? Me and my high school friends are never going to split up. We're going to be friends forever. I mean, like we might even all marry each other so we could still hang out together, you know? I mean, I think they sound as good with Cindy as they did with Florence. They're not going to break up, are they? Play a Supremes song, Cousin Brucie."

"OK kids, you want the Supremes to stay together. Let's send them a message. Beautiful Diana Ross, if you're listening, this song is from Cousin Brucie and all my listeners. 'Stop! In the Name of Love,' Diana!"

And so, in a world that is getting progressively more unrecognizable, I do my best to make everything OK between the hours of 7 and 11. Like the son of sparring parents who are clearly headed for divorce, I'm determinedly cheerful, mostly convinced that the country is just going through some growing pains. To me, this year's film sensation, The Graduate, *doesn't signal any real disenfranchisement between the adults and the kids. Mrs. Robinson is fiction, right? Those kids in the vans are just going through a phase. Besides, they're not really typical. WABC has its finger on the pulse of the nation and Herb Alpert had the number-one song, "This Guy's in Love with You," for four weeks this summer. That doesn't sound like the country is going psychedelic to me. Look at what's coming up on the charts: "Harper Valley P.T.A." You can't get more red, white, and blue than that.*

I'm thirty-two years old. I'm pulling some of the best ratings of anybody ever in modern radio. I still love what I do. TV and movies are opening to me. They're going to have to wait until I'm old enough for Social Security to get me off of WABC and away from the pulse of rock 'n' roll.

I'm going to be the one exception that proves the rule. "YEEEEEEEEEEE!" Cousin Brucie and WABC are going to go on forever. Or at least until next year.

One of the idioms of the sixties generation was "Where it's at." WABC had always been the answer to where it was at in radio. We were the last word in what was popular. But 1969 was the year that redefined where things were "at" for nearly everything that had anything to do with rock.

In August of that year the Woodstock Music and Arts Festival in Bethel, New York, was literally and figuratively the precise location of the generation that had sprung from the loins of Bill Haley, Chuck Berry, Little Richard, Elvis. The Woodstock generation sent four hundred thousand representatives to pay witness to a style of life, a kind of music, an emerging feminism, and a freedom that included free LSD, communal pond baths, and the all-time free rock concert, since only a very few of these impossibly optimistic flower children had arrived with tickets.

For three days, Woodstock was the Mount Olympus of rock 'n' roll. Hendrix, Garcia, Baez, Joplin, Cocker, Crosby, Stills, Nash, and Young joined the other gods of music in a farm field. Teachers and disciples? Rulers and subjects? One big happy family? No, there was only one acceptable identification for that congregation: the Woodstock Nation. This was Utopia. A new land that had leadership without leaders, emergency rooms without hospitals, dining rooms without restaurants, marijuana without drug busts, bedrooms without doors. It was a nation with support systems but no structure. By and large, the message of Woodstock was that it was possible for four hundred thousand people to live together without government and without fear—for a few days, anyway.

Like a psychedelic illustration, the people and events of Woodstock blur for me. Though I was an on-site reporter for WABC, and I did get in and out with the help of local police, for me, as for so many others I've spoken with since, Woodstock remains a visit to a foreign land. Like the bazaars of Morocco or the markets of Istanbul, Woodstock was sights, smells, and sounds that one sees, hears, and feels at the time, but loses in the layer upon layer of impressions that follow, until finally what you have is a composite. Much like a field of varied wildflowers or a steady rain of confetti, Woodstock doesn't yield distinguishable parts, but only a kaleidoscopic sum of music, people, color, weather, and to use the word of the times, cosmic stuff. Perhaps my perspective, that of a thirty-two-year-old emissary from the mainstream of rock, gave me as my most intense views of the event pictures of the straights from the town and the surrounding government. I wasn't surprised that the youthful attendees made do and made this impossible temporary territory work, but what I saw among the staff of the local sheriff and the state troopers was truly amazing. Along with the National Guard and the people of this tiny hamlet, the constabulary put aside any natural inclination to disapproval. They swam in that ocean of humanity seemingly on the same wavelength as their surprise visitors. It wasn't a case of If you can't beat 'em, join 'em, it was, Well, let's give it a try and see what we can learn from 'em. Perhaps the spectacles of my memory are a touch rose-colored, but I truly did go to examine the pros and cons, the downside as well as the upside of what happened in Bethel. Wandering around, I saw enough dope to reinflate the *Hindenburg,* but nothing else that came remotely close to suggesting a potential conflict between the authorities and the hippies.

Lawless. It's a word of toweringly negative connotations. Yet for a long weekend in 1968, the lawless land of Woodstock was doubly positive. Yes, it said. Yes, the rock fanatics had found the way to the summit of spontaneity. Yes, the establishment had found the way to coexist with them, if only for three days.

All of this reconciliation was all the more poignant when viewed with an eye to the biggest breakup in music history, the disbanding of the Lonely Hearts Club Band—the dissolution of the Beatles. Their breakup was as bizarre and compelling as was their debut.

In March, Ringo announced that the band would never perform in public again. That same March, Paul McCartney married Linda Eastman with no Beatles present. Also that month, John married Yoko Ono and they conducted a "bed-in for peace" in their honeymoon suite in an Amsterdam hotel. The press visited the nude couple and were treated to John and Yoko's visions of a better world. In truth, they were sincere, if uncanny, but the fans resented the exclusivity that this marriage seemed to portend. We'd expected the four Peter Pans never to grow up, never to have separate bedrooms, never to bring in someone who seemed to want to pull them apart.

Needing an explanation for John's defection, the public seized the only possible scenario. "Paul is dead," they insisted. It's not clear how the rumor started, although cynics said the Beatles wanted to play one final prank before riding off into the sunset. Soon college campuses were buzzing with the news and irrefutable evidence that began surfacing. Fans claimed that they could hear John say, "I buried Paul" during the fade of "Strawberry Fields Forever." Soon after, the album *Abbey Road* was released. Now the public was certain McCartney was no longer with us. Unlike his bandmates, Paul wore black for the cover photo and (incontrovertible!) he was barefoot. At closer inspection, one could see that George, in denim, was the gravedigger following Paul, who was preceded by Ringo, the tuxedoed undertaker, and John, the white-clad God.

Paul soon contacted the world from his home in Scotland, but, loving the drama more than Mr. McCartney, fans decided that the interview was a hoax. The frenzy continued and on the air we all left open the possibility that Paul was at least seriously ill. None of us, however, would ever do what WABC's overnight jock, Roby Yonge, did. Roby was a touch on the arrogant side, probably out of defensiveness because he was on the graveyard shift. He knew he could bend the rules a bit since management rarely monitored the station after midnight, but he'd underestimated Rick Sklar's dedication to the station and the format. At this point Rick was being hailed as a genius of rock radio. He was often kept from listening to the station, what with luncheon banquets, speaking engagements, charity balls, and the like. Still, he could listen to random selections from the continuous taping of the station and get a good idea of what was going on. He'd probably noticed Roby departing from the format, so one night he made a point of listening to a live broadcast. It was about two in the morning and what Rick heard was truly a talk show where a music show should have been.

Roby had played "Revolution 9" from the Beatles' "White Album" backward a few times and was asking listeners whether they could hear "turn me on, dead man," as some overzealous necromaniacal Beatlemaniacs had claimed. Having completely ignored station policy, Mr. Yonge was taking call after call and interjecting his "firsthand" knowledge of the Beatles. Youthful enthusiasm is part of the personality makeup of a neophyte personality radio deejay, but what Roby was doing went beyond exuberance into self-aggrandizement. Setting himself up as a kind of authority on a radio station that guarded its credibility the way Coca-Cola guarded its formula, he'd stepped over the line between unpredictability and unprofessionalism.

Rick had immediately called Les Marshak, who was then a utility jock—filling in when air personalities were ill or on vacation. "Meet me in the lobby of the ABC Building. Fast," Rick demanded. Stumbling into his clothes and half scared out of his wits, Les grabbed a taxi and met the irate Mr. Sklar within minutes.

"Roby's ignoring format," Rick shouted as his 2 A.M. greeting to Les. "You're going on." Rick filled Les in during the elevator ride to the eighth floor and made a beeline for the studio. Les sat at a live mike in the news studio and ad-libbed while Roby's mike was squelched and Rick informed him that he was off the air—for good. Rick and a security guard escorted Roby out of the studio and the building and Les went on with the statement Sklar had told him to make: "What you have heard on the air tonight is speculation. The staff and management of WABC radio and the ABC network has no firsthand knowledge of the controversy. The opinions expressed by Mr. Yonge were his own." The phones continued to light for the rest of the night, but Les was under strict orders not to answer them.

Roby may or may not have survived on WABC without the Paul project. Still, the incident underscores the continuing power of the Beatles. Even the venerable *New York Times* reported the "Paul Is Dead" mayhem, going so far as to mention that the hand shown over Paul's head on the *Sgt. Pepper* album cover was an ancient Indian death symbol while conservatively emphasizing that it seemed certain that Paul's death was a rumor without foundation. Eventually the fans soon forgot all about it.

It was, however, hard to forget about the growing strife in music. Nearly half of America's Top Forty AM stations refused to play "The Ballad of John and Yoko," which had become a very popular Beatles single. The lyrics "Christ, you know it ain't easy" were seen as offensive in markets with strict definitions of sacrilege. This wasn't the first time a song had been banned. American Indians had demanded (successfully) that the song "Indian Giver" be kept off of WABC, citing a negative stereotypical image of Native Americans as the reason. "Louie, Louie" by the Kingsmen had also been kept off of many Top Forty stations because of supposed subliminal obscenity.

Earlier in 1969, Jim Morrison of the Doors had been charged with lewd and lascivious behavior during a concert in Miami. He actually had to give himself up to the FBI in Los Angeles since he'd violated interstate laws by leaving Miami. Rock 'n' roll and rock performers were adding fuel to the fires of the Knock the Rock movement.

Jim Morrison died in 1971 while his case was on appeal. By that time death and rock were grim cohorts. Brian Jones, the Rolling Stones guitarist, was found dead in his swimming pool just weeks after his departure from the group in 1969. The Stones, whom right-wingers were calling satanic, ended the year with more tragedy. During their free "thank you" concert at Altamont Speedway in California, the Hell's Angels who'd been hired as a security force stabbed and killed one of the spectators. Eerily, California was also the setting for the most sensational and grisly deaths of the sixties. In August 1969, Charles Manson and his "family" engaged in a horrifying cult ritual, murdering Sharon Tate, pregnant wife of director Roman Polanski, and several other people. The decade that had begun with the simplicity of Paul Anka, Pat Boone, and the Shirelles was ending with the kind of events those performers had never prepared us for.

In 1969 American astronaut Neil Armstrong set foot on the moon. Briefly, in the waning weekend hours on the East Coast and during Sunday prime time on the West, in the middle of the last year of the splintering sixties, the country once again became one. "One giant leap for mankind," Armstrong had said. Many a heart did leap at the thought that we could fall into step together once more. Perfect timing, that lunar leap in that summer. The decade had begun with a vital new president. Now our dead leader's wish of landing on the moon before the end of that decade had been granted. In theory we could come to the end of the sixties standing tall with the pride of a country that had accomplished what it had set out to do.

Instead, we stumbled into the seventies.

On May 4, 1970, four students at Kent State University in America's middle-of-the-road Midwest were killed by National Guard troops during an antiwar demonstration. Though this event needed to be examined and reexamined so we might see what was becoming of our nation, the people who ran AM radio stations called the song "Ohio" by Crosby, Stills, Nash and Young anti-American. WABC was among the stations that didn't play "Ohio," thereby virtually decreeing that no main-stream station would or should. Give FM radio one more point. They not only played the song, they played it often, and the song found its way onto the charts unaided by the AM band.

By the end of 1970, Jimi Hendrix and Janis Joplin, two emerging geniuses of rock, were dead and buried. Gradually it became clear that the end of the sixties was the end of an era. Hopefulness was now history. Music would no longer be the communal goodwill medium for spreading plans for a better world.

CHAPTER FIFTEEN

The Numbered Days

By the end of 1970 I knew in my heart what my head wouldn't admit for a few more years. My marriages were ending—to Susan and to the station. In the sixties we had heard repeatedly, "Don't trust anyone over thirty." Essentially that meant the world couldn't be trusted. I was finding out that my old beliefs couldn't be trusted either. The born-conservative kid from Flatbush had had his eyes opened. The radio personality who'd told kids what was happening had learned what really was happening from those kids and from their troubadours. I couldn't trust my old self. That's what it really boiled down to, and if I couldn't trust that guy anymore, how was I going to continue to live in the worlds in which he'd been comfortable?

One day in 1968 I had spontaneously fallen into step with a procession marching down Broadway. The participants, both black and white, were walking off their grief over the death of Martin Luther King. I'd never marched before. I'd barely asked myself where I stood on the issues that were dividing my country. Just as in my radio-personality life I'd treated news-casts as separate from the real broadcast—music, contests, patter—the fun part of the show, I'd thought of the news of the world as parenthetical to my life, which was largely lived on the radio.

Compelled to join that march, I'd had no idea where they were going, but I wanted to be a part of the dignified expression of sadness. As I walked, a rock was hurled. It caught me on the leg, tearing the fabric of my pants and my skin as well. Bleeding, I left the mourners and walked to the studio, my symbolic if not my real home, where I could count on the order of things. I reflected on the people for whom rocks and billy clubs and tear gas had become a way of life. I thought too of another reality I was ignoring—the guns, grenades, and bombs that were a way of life for not only American soldiers, but the people of that tiny nation very far away. It wasn't one of those life-changing moments when a person suddenly joins a mon-astery, but it was a chink in the sturdy conservative armor I'd been living in; it was an opening through which I could see daylight, a place in my mind's eye I was drawn to, no matter how much I tried to ignore it. As the seventies dawned, it began to dawn on Cousin Brucie that Kismet was about to disappear.

In 1971 John Lennon released a song called "Imagine," encouraging us to conjure up a better world. It seemed like the ultimate contradiction of what was happening at WABC. For starters, we were getting bomb scares on a regular basis. The guards would call the receptionist, who would spread the word to evacuate. We'd cue up a tape made expressly for this purpose and leave until the bomb squad told us it was safe. The WABC Bomb Task Force was a joke. It consisted of retiree security guards more afraid to find a bomb than not to. Eventually the novelty wore off the procedure and most of the air staff volunteered to stay on the air, joking among ourselves about W-A-Bomb-C. Still, the scares were a signal of a progres-sively more violent world.

True to form, Top Forty radio was spotlighting songs like "One Bad Apple" by the Osmonds. A group with a name that sounded more like FM fare, Three Dog Night, had recorded what was now the definitive AM attitude, "Joy to the World." In 1971, it was our role to be cockeyed optimists even while hostages and prisoners were dying at New York's Attica Correctional Facility. Even the place's name was a convenient euphemism. Attica wasn't merely a "facility," it was a hellhole, where Governor Rockefeller sent a squadron of one thousand state troopers and assorted peacekeepers to end the disorder. When the storming was done, thirty-eight lay dead. Simon and Garfunkel offered a Bridge over Troubled Water at the beginning of the seventies, but it was clear that it was going to take floodgates to hold back the country's coming rush of rage.

It was at about this time that a man once hauled off and hit me after an appearance. He didn't want his son listening to that filth I played on the radio, he said. One day Dan Ingram opened a fan letter and screamed. His finger had been sliced by the razor blade inside. After that, Dan would say, "Take the money and run."

The fires of rage that were burning in our nation dimmed the light of AM's stars. In the heyday of WABC, our energy had flowed out to the WABC listeners. Now the population's passionate stands on critical causes had made a mockery of the passion of WABC's performances in the name of rock 'n' roll. Somehow it seemed we were no longer relevant. When the Beatles broke up, popular music broke apart. How strange that the group that had supposedly heralded the end of rock 'n' roll had actually been its life force. Without the Beatles, rock lost its focus. We'd reached the end of "The Long and Winding Road"—their last number-one single.

The ratings were confirming the rise of FM radio and the division this created caused the rock industry to lose the punch of collectivism and fall, divided into fragments of its former glory. Rock festivals came and went, becoming paler and paler attempts to duplicate the vibrancy of Woodstock. The rift between AM and FM grew wider and wider, with AM spotlighting the Jackson 5, James Taylor, Dawn. The most popular tunes, the ones played the most on AM from 1971 to 1973, were "Joy to the World," Roberta Flack's "The First Time Ever I Saw Your Face," and "Alone Again (Naturally)," by Gilbert O'Sullivan. All enjoyed six weeks at number one; all ignored the temperament of the country just as AM was trying to do.

Meanwhile, among the living, Sid Bernstein had another iconoclastic blockbuster group called Grand Funk Railroad. The traditional music press didn't like these guys and barely acknowledged their presence. No matter. They broke the Shea Stadium ticket sales figure that had been held by the Beatles just the same. The establishment couldn't make the underground go away simply by ignoring it. A group called Iron Butterfly went gold and the Rolling Stones continued to roll, filling both the publicity and the musical gap left by the Beatles breakup. The ragamuffins of rock started the seventies by forming their own Rolling Stones Record label and released a single called "Brown Sugar," from their *Sticky Fingers* album, a mosaic of sex, drugs, booze, and blues. The song and the album reached number one on their respective charts during the same week in May of 1971.

With the exception of the Beatles, it was rare for an artist to have both the number-one single and the number-one LP. In the early days of rock this was because the markets for singles and albums were radically different. Later it was because, by and large, singles achieved stardom on AM with one set of listeners while albums were the venue of FM and its fans. The seventies Stones, though, seemed to be everywhere, and somehow they kept up their reputation as serious musicians and radicals while still managing to appeal to the less sophisticated AM listener. Maybe it was because the group was the last bastion of mystery. What was Jagger about? Macho or unisex? Androgynous or aggressively male? Neither his movie

Performance nor his marriage to Bianca Pérez Morena de Macías in 1971 solved the mystery.

It's interesting to realize that within weeks of the Stones' double dominance of the charts, another artist topped this difficult feat. Carole King, Neil Sedaka's old friend and nemesis, hit number one with two singles "It's Too Late" and "I Feel the Earth Move" as well as the album *Tapestry*.

The top-album and top-single slots were once again occupied by the same artist in February 1972. The song and LP were both titled "American Pie" and sung by Don McLean. The popularity of both Carole King and Don McLean meant something bigger than the combined sales of their hits. The meaning became clear as a Broadway musical began to break records. The show was called *Grease* and the message was that rock had been around long enough and had changed enough to inspire nostalgia. When I saw Teen Angel descend from the skies in *Grease*, I had a jolt. How could something that seemed like it had happened yesterday be a trip down memory lane? "Look at Me, I'm Sandra Dee," "Beauty School Drop-Out," "Summer Nights." The songs were anthems to anachronisms, and people were flocking to watch them be performed. The sixties had turned the fifties into ancient history by the seventies.

Not long after *Grease* opened on Broadway, a little film directed by an unknown made it big in movie theaters. With *American Graffiti*, George Lucas focused the eyes of America on the simplicity of the early sixties. A sensitive aspiring writer, Richard Dreyfuss, is haunted by the vision of a beautiful blonde (Suzanne Somers) in a white Thunderbird convertible. Knowing this is the last night in his life when he'll ever be this young, or when life will ever again be this simple, he wants to make contact with this lovely lady, a princess for the last night of his storybook days. Being in a typical American town in the early days of rock, our hero has access to his dream. There's a link that connects the drive-in restaurant, the cruising cars, the hangouts favored by hoods, the whole young population. It's the rock radio station. Even better than the station is the man of those hours—the disc jockey played poignantly by a West Coast deejay called Wolfman Jack.

American Graffiti marked a change in the status of radio personalities. That film showed both the fantasy of radio performers as magicians who could make beautiful strangers fall in love with you and the reality of them as humble humans who often worked in lonely studios and were confounded by broken refrigerators and surrounded by mounds of melting Popsicles. This film really was the Maginot Line for me, the crystal-clear moment when everything changed forever. Like the Dreyfuss character, *American Graffiti* recognized that the kings of the drag races and sweethearts of the sock hop were gone forever. And like bobby socks, D.A. haircuts, and circle pins, the personality rock jock was the stuff of scrapbooks. I felt this chilling reality in my bones. I was still number one, but there were signs that my throne was being attacked by many forces.

By 1974, in a bleak winter made even bleaker by an incomprehensible gasoline shortage, everybody in the radio industry was watching ne'er-do-well WNBC take a run at WABC. WABC was now the elder statesman of the radio sound that had originated with a fascination with all things young.

In 1968 Herb Oscar Anderson had left WABC, and filling those very big shoes was the ultimate Mr. Nice Guy, Harry Harrison. "Good morning, New York," Harry would say as if he really meant *good*. The guy loved the morning! He loved the listeners! Harry had been the midday jock on WMCA and Rick had had his ear on him for a while before Herb could no longer take the long commute in the dark or the demand of having to get up on the right side of the bed every morning. Having come to the mountain of rock and having a naturally laid-back personality, Harry never got into a star trip. Unlike Herb, he liked and understood Top Forty and he had a way of making it palatable to that huge cross-section of the city that was the New York morning audience. By 1970, Harry's morning show was 8 rating points ahead of its nearest competitor, John Gambling, with an 18. But in 1974 the country was reeling, not rocking and rolling.

A sunny morning personality was no longer as relevant as a cynical one and New Yorkers were becoming increasingly drawn to the relevance of the daybreak irreverence of Don Imus. Doing takeoffs on media ministers, Imus would play the impassioned pastor of the Bible belt, the Reverend Billy Sol Hargus. There were fractured fairy tales and Geraldo Santana Banana, all creations of Imus and his newsman sidekick, Charles McCord. But more than anything, there was the appeal of the wash-his-mouth-out-with-soap diatribes of Mr. Don Imus himself. Dan Ingram's naughtiness was child's play compared to Imus. Where Dan joked with innuendo and double entendre, Imus poked with crudeness and rudeness. It seemed as though everybody was talking about him. The population was pissed off, sick of being lied to, tired of evasive politicians and harrowing headlines. Imus was the mouthpiece of the madder-than-hell middle class. WNBC was getting noticed.

Sensing the possibility of getting into a high-stakes game, WNBC decided to go after the highest card WABC held. That was the teen-time evening show and that was mine.

Ironically, when WNBC decided to make a run at the Cousin Brucie ace in WABC's hand, they did it with a bid from the movie that had opened my eyes to the slipping image of rock jocks. They looked for the chink in my armor with a knight who'd already shown me the chink. WNBC radio was bringing the Wolfman (née Robert Smith, and the same Wolfman from *American Graffiti*) to New York to "bury me," but he wasn't a match for me yet.

WNBC spent weeks and weeks trying to create a stir in the media. Press release after press release announced that the Wolfman was out to bury me. One morning, Rick arrived at the ABC building only to find a huge tombstone at the top of the steps. COUSIN BRUCIE'S DAYS ARE NUMBERED, it said. This monument to my demise stood six feet tall, weighed hundreds of pounds, and had to be demolished before it could be removed.

Well, the Wolfman went on the air on WNBC and in eight weeks he was Pussycat Man, licking his wounds all the way back to the Left Coast.

Still, WNBC's words were prophetic. My days *were* numbered—on WABC, that is.

Chapter Sixteen

Jodie

Examining a life is like poking a *piñata*. When you try to just peek inside, all the pieces come tumbling out. Once I started examining my discomfort at being a guardian of society's status quo, everything else in my life demanded to be examined too. What I saw was someone who had carefully structured his life to make only guest appearances in the show called *Family Man*. I did relish every moment I spent with my children, and made time for many moments, but the role of devoted husband gave me trouble. What's the phrase? We grew apart. It was inevitable that Susan and I would feel that way, since nearly all of my emotional growth came in the early seventies.

Was I in a midlife crisis at this time? Who knows. It had gotten to the point where I couldn't distinguish between my crisis and my country's. At any rate, as I began to question my relationship with WABC, I faced the reality that my marriage was ending.

Susan and I split with enough mutual respect to give Dana Jon, Paige, and tiny Meri stability and a life where both mother and father were constant influences. It worked both ways. The kids were really the only constant in my life after Susan and I parted in 1973.

Would there be a woman to share my life—a life in which a nine-, seven- and two-year-old were the absolute priorities? This was a life of six-night-a-week absences. That was for starters. I wasn't yet ready to give up the appearances and television shots that were my security blanket—security being based on how many places wanted Cousin Brucie to be a part of whatever they were calling this week's celebration. Supermarket openings. Police Athletic League cookouts. Telethons. PTA meetings. I played them all in those days.

Later in 1973 my friend Rick Shapiro called me at the studio. "Arlene wants you to meet her friend, Jodie Berlin," he said. "You're going to love her. She's very, very pretty and very, very intelligent," he went on.

"How old is she?" I wanted to know. "She's *what*?" I shouted in disbelief after he told me she was a mere year younger than I. I was at the time being so original as to date girls so far my junior they could have accurately been labeled "girlettes." My usual companions were long-haired cheerleader types who sipped daiquiris and smiled. They weren't exactly Fulbright Scholars, but after the subliminal sparring that precedes most divorces, I was avoiding emotional challenges at all costs.

What would I say to this Jodie person? I'd have to "make conversation." I'd have to listen. Respond. Behave like a grown-up, in other words. I wasn't sure I wanted to go through that much trouble for anyone. "You're going to love her," Rick insisted. "She's one of the few truly happy people I know."

One of the truly happy. This I had to see.

The rest, as they say, is history. One evening with that special woman, who truly did seem to be content, and I was a goner. I'd make conversation forever, if she'd promise to be there.

The first night I took Jodie out, we went to an Italian restaurant in Little Italy. It was the start of a routine that alternated pasta with Oriental food. Chinese restaurant. Italian restaurant. Jodie and I took a chance apiece at selecting our dining places. (I would have probably even eaten tofu to be with her, but thankfully it hadn't yet become a culinary craze.)

One night about a year and a half after we'd met, I took Jodie to the Sum Hey Rice Shoppe in Chinatown. This was where we frequently ate after I got off the air. I left Jodie at "our" table, and went to talk with the waiter. He spoke very little English. I speak "menu" Chinese. With the help of hand gestures, smiles, and eye rolling, he understood. He would tuck the piece of paper I'd handed him into a fortune cookie and give it to the lady when our meal was over.

The message read MY DARLING JODIE, WILL YOU MARRY ME?

Jodie screamed. She cried. She shrieked. She ran to the pay phone to call her girlfriend. I figured that meant yes.

We felt determined to do the most hopeful thing two people can do—join their lives together. So on December 26, 1974, Ms. Berlin and I had the most memorable day of our lives.

> If I could save time in a bottle
> If words could make wishes come true.
> I'd save every day till eternity passes away.
> Just to spend them with you.

So went the words to the number-one song on that day. It was a posthumous hit for Jim Croce and it was exactly how I felt.

Twenty friends gathered to witness our wedding. Dana Jon was my best man. Paige was the maid of honor. The ceremony was simple, brief. It was as simply beautiful and simply meaningful as my bride herself. Jodie needed no fanfare, no ceremonial attention, no outlandish production. She was (and continues to be) so supremely at peace with herself that she made a celebration of the privacy of moments. So we had a very private wedding and I received the greatest luxury of my life to date. A private life at last.

Anything I choose to say about Jodie and the life we share sounds impossibly corny to me. It's just that I was ready to "share" in every sense of that word. Where once I'd felt I had to be the last word in all decisions, I began to relish making decisions with a partner. Where once I demanded a formal home, I began to learn the subtleties of the country craftsmanship that Jodie so loved. When she realized her lifelong dream of opening an antiques shop, I became her partner in a new way—refinishing, schlepping, relishing the buying trips and the "finds" in little out-of-the way places.

I liked Italy better with Jodie there to share my linguine. Paris became even more lovely with her by my side. My beloved Jamaica took on a new magic. Gradually, I didn't need the city glitter all the time. Maine was as romantic as any South Sea island. I came to cherish the quiet life with someone I loved being quiet with.

Bruce Meyerowitz, the kid who had always been independent because at an early age he had what the other kids had not yet gotten—a career dream—finally had something he never knew he'd wanted: a best friend.

Another wonderful thing happened. I learned that Bruce Morrow didn't have to be Cousin Brucie all the time. The woman I married accepted herself completely and accepted me completely too—the off-the-air me included. To this day Jodie isn't what one would call a Cousin Brucie fan. That guy is a little too frantic for her tastes. She seems to favor plain old Bruce Morrow.

Plain old Bruce Morrow. In 1973, he was a guy I was terrified of. By 1974, I had to take the chance of being him full time. I had to risk leaving the place that had made Cousin Brucie what the radio industry called "a legend."

I had to leave WABC.

CHAPTER SEVENTEEN

The End of the Beginning

Most people will tell you that the early rock songs were incomparably naïve, but 1974 certainly gave them a run for their money. What could be more childish than a song about running around in the altogether? Yes, 1974 gave us both the fad and the anthem called "The Streak." Ray Stevens stayed at the top of the charts for three weeks with the tune that was country rock if it was anything. After taking our musical cues from Great Britain for so long, perhaps we were ready to turn to our country roots for inspiration, but what we got with the infusion of country into rock was uninspired. "Billy Don't Be a Hero" was a case in point. John Denver chimed in with "Sunshine on My Shoulders" and "Annie's Song," smiling and shouting "Far out!" at every opportunity. Yes, by the fourth year of the seventies, the "heads" had disappeared and the mainstream types were co-opting their lingo.

We were a weary nation. Each day brought news that carried the onus for the Watergate swindle closer and closer to the office occupied by Tricky Dicky. In the past, our country had experienced times that were just as disillusioning, but never with the eye of television staring at the proceedings. The children of the media, the kids who'd been the energy of the sixties, were being treated to the mean side of their technological baby-sitter.

We were a long, long way from Uncle Miltie and Buffalo Bob.

I heard the phrase "corporate rock" for the first time in 1974. Sleek. Controlled. Goal-oriented. Such was the stuff of the "corporate" sound. It was the kind of music that threatened no one. It was significant that the word *corporate* was being used in conjunction with *rock*. Rock had become pinstriped. And the pinstriped types were driving me nuts. With pap papering the charts, the office guys who had been afraid to do anything but hang on to the radio rock rocket now felt free to tinker with things. You can imagine how top-heavy with tinkerers a corporation like the ABC network was. The Sons of Business were having a field day. The more frequently I received memos from Sklar and the higher-ups, the more sure I was that it wouldn't be long before the neophytes got around to noodling with the air staff. Still, they sneaked up on me.

One day Rick invited me into his office to discuss an "interesting deal."

I was sure I was on to what he wanted to discuss. Pat Whitley had been trying to convince me to go to WNBC, the station, remember, that had brought Wolfman Jack to New York to "bury Cousin Brucie." Pat was the program director of WNBC, and together with Perry Bascom, the vice-president and general manager of the station, had been romancing me with promises of complete autonomy, *"the kind of freedom you used to have on WABC, Bruce."* We'd met surreptitiously in dark restaurants and in the subterranean niches in the bowels of Rockefeller Center, home of most of the NBC studios and offices. When Rick mentioned an "interesting deal," I thought my cover had been blown. Now WABC was going to make an offer to put a stop to the WNBC seduction.

Rick squirmed and paced as he began his pitch. Why was he

so nervous? I wondered. Just tell me how much more money you're willing to pay for my continued loyalty, I thought, and then let me tell you that it isn't money I'm looking for, it's the sense of abandon I used to have.

"Bruce, I've got a deal for you," Rick began. "A way for you to make some more money." He loved the generous-uncle role. Why wasn't he looking at me?

"We're going to establish a ratings base and salary base for you and then pay you an additional five thousand dollars for each point you go up in the ratings."

"And if I go down, Rick?" Remember what was happening in New York radio. Where previously the predictable AM stations shared the radio audience, the now-powerful FM stations were making inroads among the listeners and further splintering the radio market, which was already dividing the audience dozens of ways. The young who had always tuned to Cousin Brucie to hear what was happening were now hearing "corporate rock" on my tightly formatted show. If they wanted the progressive stuff, they'd have to go to stations with progressive management—FM stations. There was no way the highest-rated AM station was going to go up in the ratings.

"If you go down, it'll be a five-thousand-dollar deduction for every point."

I had always thought I was born under a lucky star, but it wasn't until that fateful meeting in Rick Sklar's office that I understood the magnitude of that star. By this time, Sid Bernstein, the visionary who'd brought the Beatles to the States, was my agent. When WNBC had started talking to me, Sid had reminded me that it was going to be very costly to move. *Unless I could get WABC to release me from my contract.*

"No way I'm going to agree to that proposition, unless we talk about every aspect of my contract, Rick," I stated with all the conviction I wasn't feeling. "Cancel my contract and let's negotiate a new one. Then you and Sid and I can talk compensation structures."

One week later, my contract with WABC was canceled and I

was no longer bound by the constraints that were designed to keep me from switching stations. WABC wanted to discuss tying my compensation to the ratings of a station and a radio band that was sure to lose ratings. There was nothing to discuss. WNBC and I had already sewn up our deal and the only thing I had to say to the management of WABC was good-bye.

At about this time the movie theaters of Manhattan were playing a movie that had all the beautiful bittersweetness of the films of days gone by. *The Way We Were* was a tearjerker about a nice Jewish girl (Barbra Streisand) who simply can't stop campaigning for justice. "People *are* their principles," she insists. Her not-so-nice Gentile husband (Robert Redford), who "was a lot like the country he was born in—things came too easily for him," doesn't understand why she has to make things so hard for herself. I felt as though I were playing both roles. Things had come almost too easily for me. Still, I was leaving "home" because of my principles. I would never lie to my listeners. Pretending that the show I was forced to do under the strict rules of the 1974 version of WABC was "movin' and a-groovin', havin' a ball with Cousin Brucie" was a lie.

Rick and the pinstripes in the big offices were shocked. Cousin Brucie on another station? Unthinkable. Surely there was an offer I would take. No, there was no offer that would make me change my mind. I'd gotten the one message that would turn me away from my beloved WABC. You're only as good as your ratings. Forget history, forget loyalty, forget everything but the numbers. I was out of there. If business was business, I had to make a business decision. It was clear that WNBC was going to give me the latitude to run my own show.

Rules are made to be broken, and in the case of Cousin Brucie's departure, WABC shattered the rule that says you never let a jock go on the air to say good-bye. WABC in particular was strict about denying disgruntled soon-to-be-ex-employees access to their powerful microphones. Bill "Roscoe" Mercer's on-air resignation after Murray the K had been fired from WOR-FM in 1967 might just serve as further proof that jocks should not be left on the air if there was any possibility of their using the station's access to the public to make a personal point. In fact, the FCC specifically forbids personal messages on the air. Ironically, Bill Mercer reenacted his flaunting of the rules again in 1986. Broadcasting on a New York City station with a heavy black audience, he told listeners that recent program changes were racially motivated. Soon after that statement, Roscoe Mercer was fired.

Of course there are charming ways to flaunt the FCC no-personal-statement rule. Dana Jon's birth is a case in point. And Les Marshak bent the rule in a most beautiful way for an extremely beautiful lady. For a few weeks, Les devoted a portion of his daily morning show on WPIX-FM to an elaborate continuing drama. He had gotten his listeners involved in the adventures of Morton and Beatrice. This was all Les's fanciful way of leading up to a marriage proposal to his mesmerizing girlfriend, Nancy, whom he'd told to listen to his show that morning and who, hearing Morton ask Beatrice to be his bride, immediately called the station to say yes. Obviously, stations and the FCC look the other way for happy events, but the rule is when a jock decides to leave he never gets to say good-bye. Why was WABC going to break this rule?

First of all, they knew I'd never do anything to hurt the station that had been the impetus and the stage for my maturation as a radio personality. Second of all, since WNBC was making a huge deal out of my joining them, WABC wasn't about to relinquish my listeners without a fight. They built up "Cousin Brucie's Last Broadcast on WABC" as if it were a happy celebration they'd thought up. Behind the scenes, they prepared a farewell bash. Barely understanding the impact of what was about to happen, I went through the next few days in a daze.

During the weeks before high school graduation, one's eyesight changes. It's as if you've got this bionic power to look at things and run little movies of how they figured in the most gauzy, lovely, happy days of your life. "That locker, old number two forty-five," you say to yourself. "How many hours did my buddy and I spend leaning on that locker salivating over the girls in their cardigans?" Imagine then a high school you went to for thirteen years, a school where they paid you to have a good time. A school where the principal and teachers stayed away from you and the kids ran everything. Imagine, if you can, the emotions you'd have when it was time to graduate from this utopian institution. Such were the emotions I brought to the night that was going to be my last as a WABC air personality.

Tingling with sadness, fear, and the dread of the unknown, I walked into the broadcast studio. The bionic movies started. This was the studio where I'd had my *Saturday Night Party*. How many "date nights" had I spent in this room, watching Billys and Janets jitterbug as if there were no tomorrow? How many pizzas and Cokes had I consumed in the name of being "one of the gang"? How many kids had fallen in love in this studio? And how many had fallen in love while listening to the broadcasts that had originated here? Talk about rock 'n' roll heaven—Elvis, Buddy Holly, Chuck Berry, Diana Ross and her Supremes, John, Paul, George, and Ringo—they'd all been here. All I had to do was rub the magic turntable and they'd drift in, musical genies granting our every wish. "In the Still of the Night," the all-time make-out song, how many times had I played that one right here in this studio?

Better not to think about that. What's past is past and even if I could bring back the kids, the pizzas, the listeners, I couldn't change what was happening in music. Incredibly, it had become fashionable to be called a punk. Punks used to be troublemakers, the guys you wouldn't dare bring home. Now a group called the Ramones was being hailed as a rock breakthrough, and the more angry the music sounded the better it supposedly was. As bad as that was, nothing could be worse than the plastic sound of disco. Musak for the brain dead, that's what it sounded like. All you needed was a whistle and lyrics that would kill a diabetic and you were a disco star.

It was probably a good thing that I was leaving. I needed to shake myself up a bit; I needed to create change in order to cope with change.

Just a few doors down from the broadcast studio, a Cousin Brucie party *was* in progress. Tonight, though, instead of the usual pepperoni-pie feast, there was a spread that looked as though the station were going to try to block my exit by erecting a wall of comestibles. More accurately, it was like a wake. The family of the deceased shows how much he meant to them by having the food signify love. The living affirm their aliveness by eating. Everybody speaks in loud voices, as if the dear departed can hear them via some invisible long-distance phone line. Every once in a while somebody breaks down and weeps. The event is punctuated by tears and laughter, the most basic of all our communication skills. Cousin Brucie's farewell banquet was like that with two exceptions. The "departed" was present. So was Howard Cosell.

The secret of *The Wizard of Oz* is that you don't need what you think you need, you only need evidence of what you've had all along. The tin man, it turns out, doesn't need a heart; he needs a testimonial. I certainly didn't feel like I needed the testimonial that was being staged for me. Only a tin head could have withstood the pain of feeling so close to so many people who feel so close to you too. It was like one of those smarmy Christmas weeks when all the co-workers feel benevolent to each other. We indulged our most sentimental selves that night. All of us except The Mouth, that is.

Part of the evening's proceedings was a "This Is Your Life, Cousin Brucie." Leave it to Rick—even a party had to have a format. By and large, the events and people that were conjured up were sweet, silly, touching. Then Cosell came on. Not content to simply be a bit player in this show, Cosell had prepared a "roast." The tone was completely alien to what was going on, but that would have been OK if only Howard had kept things cute instead of cutting. Cosell lambasted me. My career was a sham, was the essence of what he said. I was nothing without Rick Sklar, he said (how many brownie points was he trying to score with that one?). He went on about how he had made Dandy Don Meredith and how Dandy Don would go into oblivion on WNBC and so would I. It was a cutting, caustic, self-serving performance. One that shifted the tone from affectionate ribbing to insensitive skewering. Cosell was obviously at a loss, speaking not of sports, but of things that truly meant something to the people in the room. Howard's heartless send-off blew a chill wind through my already breaking heart.

Somehow someone smoothed over Cosell's remarks and the evening went on. I had one more piece of evidence that it was time for me to leave. The atmosphere that was taking away people's self-respect was also making it impossible for people to respect each other. Where Mr. Cosell and I had once been respectful colleagues, if not downright comrades, we now were behaving the way people do when things get chaotic. "Every man for himself" was the message I got from my roast a la Howard.

Then, with the event still in full swing, it was time to go on the air. The first indication that I was going to have trouble that night came when I looked at Dan. He stood at the mike and looked at me as if to say, "You're not really going to go through with this, are you?"

"Okay, kemosabe, it's all yours," he finally said. Always the consummate pro, there was no way Dan was going to intrude on my private farewell by questioning my decision.

The next hurdle came when I had to face Saul Rochman, the engineer. He had my jingle cued up and ready to go. The commercials were neatly stacked, ready to be played when the log dictated. Everything was just as it always was. Except for the sadness on his face. A brief hug, a quick glance away, I walked to the stool to begin the end.

"Well, cousins, it's your Cousin Brucie, doing his last broadcast on WABC. We've made a whole lot of memories in the past thirteen years, haven't we?

Let's make tonight the best memory of all. Let's see,
I don't have to do the format tonight, do I? So let me
play the first song I ever played on WABC—'Maybelline,' by Cousin Chuck Berry!"

The mike given over to the record, I sat up a little straighter
and cleared my throat. This wasn't going to be easy. I reached
for the next tune I wanted to play. How about "Hey Jude"?
"Hey Jude, don't make it bad—take a sad song and make it
better." Leave it to the Beatles to have the right thing to say. I
spun the cartridge rack and pulled it out without looking at the
label. Oh God, was everything going to feel like a beloved
memory tonight? How many times had I played the pick-the-
cartridge game with the jocks? We were all always vying for the
title of "Fastest Jock in the East," perfecting our techniques for
finding a cartridge without having to scan the labels, having
memorized its number and its place on the rack. Would this
game, like stoopball and dirt war, be now relegated to a place
in the past?

That's what this departure was, after all, wasn't it? A kind of
growing up. I had thought of WABC as my family. When they
tried to treat me like an employee, I had balked. Still, on this
night it felt like I was going away from home. Forever.

Then the phones started. At first, I was into what good radio
this was. The fans involved, just as I always liked them to be,
the frenzy of handling the show, the log, the calls, all at the
same time—*this* was the kind of show I loved. Except for the
topic on everybody's minds.

"How can you leave WABC, Cousin Brucie? I feel as if I'm
being betrayed."

"First the Dodgers move away from Brooklyn and now
this. . . . What's the world coming to? All anybody cares about
is money."

"Things will never be the same."

At first I liked hearing that I was going to be missed, but after
only a short while I realized I couldn't take it. I couldn't take the

229

responsibility of disappointing people. "What about me?" I wanted to shout, but instead I commiserated with them, I told them it was time. I talked about "growing apart." I had only clichés to offer; there was nothing clever to be said.

After about two hours of trying to keep the show together, I had to admit it was out of control. I didn't know when to play a record, when to give Saul a commercial cue, when to segue into the news. For the first time in my life I let the show get away from me.

How ironic that that night was when I learned why a show needs a structure. Every show is a skyscraper under construction. You can't complete the building unless you have a framework. You can't add a sixteenth floor unless you've got the skeleton for the fifteenth. I was working without a framework that night. I was also working without a net. I was, for the first time on the air, afraid. I was afraid of falling—apart.

Chuck Leonard was just sort of hanging out before his shift, which was to begin after mine, splitting his time between the party in the big studio and my broadcast down the hall. He peeked in every now and then to give me the high sign and see how I was doing. Finally I admitted that I wasn't doing very well and I asked him if he'd take over the show. Solemnly he nodded and quickly, choking with sadness, I said good-bye.

"Well, my dear, dear cousins . . . it seems I can't continue. This is perhaps the saddest day of my career. We have been together for many years and I will always remember your loyalty and affection. I must leave now, but I promise you all, we shall be together again very soon. Good night, my cousins. Good night, my friends. Good night."

And so it ended. An era. An identity. A passion. I would never be Cousin Brucie of WABC again. I would never do it all for love again. Chime time. Seventy-seven, WABC. Principal of the Year. Scraps of a career to be pasted in a scrapbook. Brucie introduces the Beatles at Shea Stadium. Brucie in his leopard-skin tux at Palisades Park. Brucie, Rick, and the ridiculous kite contest. Brucie throwing a bag of underwear at Dan Ingram. While I was at ABC, this was who I was. The night I said good-bye they became who I used to be.

Nineteen seventy-four. Richard Nixon became the first president ever to resign. Gerald Ford was sworn in as the thirty-eighth Commander in Chief. Ford pardoned Nixon. Nelson Rockefeller became our vice-president. MSFB featuring the Three Degrees hit number one with "TSOP" (The Sound of Philadelphia)." Anything could happen. I walked out of the WABC building on August 7, 1974, never to return. Anything had.

CHAPTER EIGHTEEN

The N in End

In America's red, white, and blue banner year, the country that had defined itself in terms of what rolled out of the General Motors and Ford plants, was straying from Detroit. Imported cars were eagerly embraced by the formerly passionate children of the sixties. Where once a low-to-the-ground speedster or funky van had been the goal, a sturdy Saab, Volvo, or similarly hardy car was now a prestigious possession. It was a time of putting substance before form.

It was fascinating that this development happened just about when we were being served heaping portions of patriotism. The Bicentennial was a larger-than-life event that defined citizenship for us. Everywhere we turned we were bombarded by birthday blather.

We also had a show-stopping Bicentennial surprise up our sleeve. We were going to prove that one of our most sentimental beliefs—that America was the country where anybody could grow up to be president—was true. We were going to elect a nobody to the post.

232

James Earl "Call Me Jimmy" Carter seduced us with the one line that was sure to win us over. Humbly he would introduce himself to whatever crowd was assembled, be it six people sitting on the front porch of a general store or sixty million watching on TV. "Hello, I'm Jimmy Carter and I'm running for president," he'd say. Then he'd deliver the killer line. "I will never lie to you." That simple statement was music to our ears after the agony the determined deceivers in the Nixon administration had put us through. One had only to look at the charts to see that we'd fall like a rock from the top of the Empire State Building for Mr. Peanut's honest face and eagle-scout reputation. In 1976 Paul Simon reached number one with "Fifty Ways to Leave Your Lover," the Four Seasons resurfaced with "December, 1963 (Oh, What a Night)," Johnnie Taylor's "Disco Lady" was a blockbuster, as was "Silly Love Songs" by McCartney and Wings. We weren't exactly seeking out breakthrough thinking; we pretty much wanted simplicity.

Mr. Carter certainly was the embodiment of that.

If rock was seeking a way to pledge its allegiance, it had to do nothing more than note that one group bookended 1976 with two platinum albums, one in February, the other in December. The group's name? The Eagles. It was probably strictly coincidence that the country rockers shared their name with the national symbol, but it did provide a nice symmetry to the year.

Come with me to November 1976:

"So, my friends, it's a November noontime. What's for lunch? Got any hamburgers? Or chicken soup? Mmmmmmm, a nice meatloaf for lunch. Why don't you call your Cousin Brucie on WNBC and give me the answer to this question. Where did Abba get their name? One of the most successful groups in the world, probably the most successful right now, Abba. Where did their name come from?"

The phones light up immediately. Ah, my audience has gotten a bit older, but they haven't lost their touch. I remember several years ago a girl told me that she dialed the WABC contest number and then left her finger in the dial at the last number. When a contest was

233

announced, (often an hour later) all she had to do was take her finger out of the dial and presto, she was one of the first callers. Even if I asked for caller number twenty-five, the listeners had to be lightning-fast to beat out the battalions tuned to 77 on their AM dials.

Even in these touch-tone times, they still have it. A housewife from Queens correctly answers that the name Abba came from the first letter of each of the group members' first names. She wins a dinner for two at a midtown Manhattan restaurant. I don't ask the actual names. I can't name them unless I'm reading from an album cover. Anni-Frid, Benny, Björn, Agnetha. They're a long way from John, Paul, George, and Ringo, just as everything seems to be, with disco trashing the charts and punkers like the Sex Pistols shooting holes in the old formulas.

It's not surprising that it's a schizophrenic time for popular music. America has two generations of rock fans for the first time ever. The people who grew up loving Elvis are about thirty-five years old. The fifteen-year-old kids of today know the early Presley the way the kids of the fifties knew Bing Crosby—as a bit of history.

My Queens housewife probably wept when Elvis became a soldier. Today she's nearly weeping for joy.

"Thank you, Cousin Brucie, thank you. This is just great. I haven't been out to dinner in months."

"Well, you're going to go out compliments of your favorite radio station. What's your favorite station?"

"WNBC."

"That's right. Home of Imus in the Morning. Don't forget now— you promised to make a hamburger for me."

"I won't forget. Bye, Cousin Brucie."

I'm probably talking about hamburger because midday feels like chopped chuck to me. Evenings are lean, prime sirloin. Home of the streamlined youth. Full-tilt energy. But WNBC, the station that promised me the 7 to 11 P.M. freedom to be the old Cousin Brucie, has put me where Cousin Brucie has never been, nor ever wanted to be— 10 A.M. to 2 P.M. They want to follow their Peck's Bad Boy, Don Imus, with sunshine. They know that Don is a gold mine for them, but they're not really comfortable with the innuendo and nearly slanderous *approach to anything sacred. Nobody and nothing escape the barbs of iconoclastic Mr. Imus.*

I'm now filling the position of contrast to Don. Listeners not only hear the contrast—if they come to Rockefeller Center they can see it.

When the Rockefeller family used their money to build their great Art Deco city-within-a-city that is home to office buildings, broadcast studios, restaurants, a post office, a passport office, a plethora of shops, a subway stop, airline offices, and the bucolic skating rink over which the city's official Christmas tree presides every winter, they truly considered the bruised human spirit of Depression America. It was as if they wanted to give the downtrodden an access to money, to grandeur, to grace. In a spirit of access, the National Broadcasting Company—NBC—provided tours for the public. One could be treated to a glimpse of the makeup room where such luminaries as Dave Garroway and Johnny Carson were primped for the cameras. People could peek into the studios where Strike It Rich *and* Playhouse 90 *were broadcast live across the country. Equally intriguing, tourists could see what they usually could only hear. The WNBC radio broadcast studio had a large glass window, which, when the curtains were open, gave people a view of whatever radio personality was on the air. They still do.*

Broadcasting during the tour rush hours, I sit on display like those people who used to sleep in department-store windows trying to win a suite of furniture. I'm an old hand at this. I've broadcast from many a public place in my time and I've presided over the toughest glass booth in America—Irving Rosenthal's Palisades Park goldfish bowl. Rather than looking up to see a gaggle of giggling teenaged girls swooning over the latest Fabian, I'm now sometimes jolted by the stares of convention wives sporting badges that inevitably say something like PRE-STRESSED CONCRETE CONVENTION. HI! I'M MADGE! *Every once in a while I cue the engineer, lean back, swirl in my swivel chair, and meet the gaze of dozens of camera-clad Japanese businessmen, probably in America to determine how to cash in on our abandonment of the U.S. auto industry.*

Veteran of the Dramatic Workshop, drone of the NYU radio station, declared legend of the most popular radio station in the history of

*American radio, sought-after personality of the revitalized WNBC, I
cannot close the curtains. It seems as though it is my responsibility to
give the tourists a view of a living, breathing cog in the great radio
wheel. I've taken my fuel, my energy, from people like Madge and
Sadaharu there. I can at least give them a view of me in return. Imus
feels differently and keeps the curtain closed. I think it's because he's
shy, and prefers the anonymity of being a faceless voice.*

*Maybe I keep the curtains open because I know that I won't be
working as a hired jock much longer. Maybe I still believe in the magic
of the box that talks. The reason isn't important. Cousin Brucie has
stepped over a line of some sort. It's a decision that makes me feel
untouchable.*

*The window poses no threat. The threat is inside of me. It is
burnout.*

When I got to WNBC I soared the way any honeymooner
does. Heralded by an ad campaign that told the whole city
GOOD MOVE, COUSIN BRUCIE, I spent my first year at the station as
if it were my first year in the business. The fans responded as
if they were hearing rock radio for the first time. From 7 to 11
P.M., the shows were the way they used to be—juggling acts,
with phones lighting up, dedications piling up, and commercials adding up. It was what we all want to believe in forever,
that every promise anyone ever makes to you will be kept.

But of course that can't happen.

The first indication that the promises were going to be broken
came after about a year, when John Lund, one of a succession of
WNBC program directors, handed me a book called *Future Shock*.
He said it had something to do with his plans for *my* future. A
week later I was on at midday, "Housewife Heaven." When I left
the air after this shift I felt gritty. Leaving the station in the
daylight, I felt as though I were cheating somebody. Why wasn't
I getting ready to go to work?

But if the NBC peacock wanted me at midday, I'd play at
midday—that was my attitude. One way I played was with
"parades":

TAPED ANNOUNCER: "And now, let's join Cousin Brucie on the Corner of Fifty-first Street and Fifth Avenue for live parade coverage. . . . Cousin Brucie, Come in!" (SOUND EFFECTS: CROWD, PARADE NOISES)

"Thank you, Al, this is truly a great day here in New York City and yes, we have another special imaginary parade for you." (SOUND EFFECTS: HELICOPTER LANDING) "Just a minute, ladies and gentlemen. Bobby, give me some more cable. I want to get closer. Yes, yes, cousins . . . it's the mayor's helicopter landing on the steps of St. Patrick's. He's getting out. Well, well, he looks terrific in that Easter bunny outfit. His little tail is twitching. Mr. Mayor? Mr. Mayor, we're here live on the air on W-NNNNN-B-C. What have you got to say to the listeners?" (BRUCIE COVERS MOUTH WITH HAND AND SQUEAKS) "And happy Easter to you too, Mr. Mayor. Al Brady, I'll send it back to you, there are thousands and thousands of people out here today and the police want me to move the mobile unit out of the way."

I repeatedly stressed the "imaginary" aspect of the parades after I learned a lesson with the first one I'd broadcast. It was really the fulfillment of a long-held desire, a complete radio parade with bands, floats, luminaries. I described the parade queen and her lovely entourage, felt sentimental when the veterans marched by in uniform, loved the high school bands (especially the ones with white tubas), and the march music—so moving. I could see that this parade was going to go on quite awhile; it seemed endless. Give the city a parade and you give them not only a reasonable excuse for the ridiculous traffic jams, but a delicious din to counteract the noisome atmosphere that prevails on most days. Give them a description of the most colorful celebration to come down Fifth Avenue in a long, long while and the citizens are going to come out to try to catch a little of the spirit. Several hundred came to that first parade, came looking for the reviewing stand outside Rockefeller Center, and saw only the springtime display of flowers on the promenade and the pretzel vendors on the sidewalks. They were disappointed. They were even what could be called angry. Many of them decided to take this up with Cousin Brucie and began gathering in the marbled lobby of the NBC building.

The station security force came into the broadcast studio and told me they were going to escort me out through the basement that day. A car waited outside the building and I made a guilty getaway, secretly delighted that I'd pulled that one off so successfully. Midday could be exciting after all. I had midday and more.

I had struck a deal with WNBC to do regular entertainment features on *NewsCenter 4*, the hour-long local TV newscast. I spent the afternoons and evenings interviewing the cadre of celebrities that came to New York, music's Mecca.

Ella Fitzgerald one day, Liberace or Kinky Friedman and the Texas Jew Boys the next, I went from the sublime to the ridiculous, my trusty cameraman/magician, Wing Lee, by my side.

Some interviews were like wrestling with a stick of dynamite. The divine Ms. M lit the fuse to one of *NewsCenter 4*'s most explosive segments. Petite and compact, Bette Midler was wearily watching yet another camera crew set up yet another forest of lights, umbrellas, cables, and cameras on the stage of the Westchester Premier Theatre. The interviewer, known for his own brand of zaniness, empathized with the compact performer, who was required to be taller on stage than she must feel in real life. I downplayed the first few questions, thinking to give her a cushy time of it. This interview didn't have to be a performance. Besides, there was something to be said for giving the audience a glimpse of the sensitive side of the lady.

"So, the shy girl from Hawaii makes it big. Tell me, Bette, how did you get your start?"

"Are you going to ask the same bullshit everybody else does? I'm surprised at you, Cousin Brucie!"

Lights, camera, action—reflexes for the woman who called her backup group the Harlettes. I held on for my life as the next twenty minutes of tape twirled in the magic wand of Midler's might. Working the other side of the microphone, I had something to learn—sometimes performing is the only way a performer wants to be seen. For the public, for the time, Bette Midler's outrageousness *was* her personality. Her energy was her temperament. The sensitive, tired side was for the time and place where no cameras rolled, where no one watched.

Fast on the heels of Marvelous Midler came an interview with a true goddess of rock 'n' roll. She was eating Spam, oranges, and crackers when I arrived in her suite at the Waldorf-Astoria. Standing aloof from me and the crew, the lady's husband and performing partner preferred to wait until the cameras were rolling before he would deign to speak. The woman, on the other hand, was outgoing, gracious, and probably glad to have the company, given what a stiff her spouse seemed to be. For my part, I didn't care if he participated in the segment or not. Actually, I would have been satisfied to run four minutes of the lady's legs. Such were my emotions when visiting Proud Mary herself—Tina Turner.

One more lady stands out. She was tiny. She was sweet. She had a lot of gospel songs in her repertoire. She was someone called Pat Benatar. She was a natural. As the cameras rolled, she talked about always wanting to be a singer. She was respectful of the roots of rock music and talked of how much she'd learned from listening to the great balladeers. Her original stuff was a surprise. Rather than mimicking the styles she so admired, she wrote songs that didn't reflect any recognizable heritage.

When we edited the more than twenty minutes of film into the measly four minutes we had available to us, we were torn between having her talk and letting her sing. We offered as much of each as we could and sent the film to the news studio with a prayer for its safe journey into the hearts of the viewers. The back of Pat's first album tells the story of what happened next.

With Pat Benatar I branched into the more experimental music forms. On·*NewsCenter 4* I was a music reporter, not an AM jock, free to report whatever was happening in music. For a while what was happening was a large phenomenon named Meat Loaf. He said I should feel free to call him "Meat." That interview, done in 1978, was combined with an eerie visual interpretation of *Bat Out of Hell*, which Mr. Loaf had produced. Special creepy effects and wild staging that look tame in comparison with any of the videos produced in the eighties were innovative in those days.

I was getting hooked on the TV gig; free-lancing fever was burning in me. At WABC I'd had some renegade moments—a few summers playing around on the drag-racing circuit, a producing venture with my dad that produced the Eternals with "Bobaloo's Wedding Day" and the Genies with "Who's That Knockin' " and Project 42, a youth marketing consulting division of Leiber Katz Paccione advertising—but always the station had intervened and explained that walking the straight and narrow was the way to continue on the path to my career success. Going to WNBC had represented a return to the renegade side of myself, but, in time, WNBC's true colors weren't much different from those of WABC. John Lund was eventually fired, and as America entered its third century, Cousin Brucie entered his third decade on radio—a long, long time.

Long enough for a legend to die.

The death of Elvis Presley in August 1977 was a turning point on the radio road. Elvis had anchored AM radio. A look at some *Billboard* statistics shows the following about the king. Of the top one hundred records from 1955 to 1984, Elvis has the winner, "Don't Be Cruel"/"Hound Dog," a two-sided hit that stayed at number one for 11 weeks and stayed on the charts for 28. "All Shook Up" is the seventh most popular recording, number one for 9 weeks and on the charts for 30. Thus Elvis is the only artist to have two of the top ten records in the thirty years of contemporary radio. Ten records in the top one hundred are his. The Beatles have but four. Of the records making the Top Forty for 22 weeks or more, Elvis is the only one to have three. Elvis occupies the number-one slot in the following categories: Most Top Ten Records (38), Most Weeks in Number One Position (80), Most Charted Records (107!). The Beatles edge him out in Most Number One Records with 21; Elvis has 18. By giving points for various chart positions and weeks on the charts, *Billboard* came up with a figure representing the popularity of the top artists between 1955 and 1984. Elvis won with 5,131. His nearest competitor? The Beatles, with 2,940 points.

Rolling Stone reports that Elvis Presley's recording of Paul Anka's "My Way" went gold five months after his death. It became the seventy-eighth of his records to make the top twenty-five. (Ironically, in 1978.) The day after Elvis died, Jimmy Carter issued a statement from the White House. "Elvis Presley's death deprives our country of a part of itself. He was unique and irreplaceable. His music and his personality . . . changed the face of American popular culture. His following was immense and he was a symbol to people the world over, of the vitality, rebelliousness and good humor of his country."

I think of the voice, so familiar, at the other end of the telephone line in 1959. It was a polite young man calling from Memphis. "I just want to thank you for playing my records, sir," came the words clad in southern tones that sounded the way velvet feels. "I sure do appreciate it." The short conversation (instigated by Colonel Parker, no doubt, and duplicated to dozens of stations, I'm sure) left me feeling like the keeper of a treasure. Grown so far from the Elvis the Pelvis days, he hadn't grown too big for his britches. The country boy had a friend in the big city.

Elvis had been our king, our musical ambassador, our assurance that the American dream could come true. When he died he took some of our hope with him. Radio was the only safe public place for the man whose popularity had exiled him to the life of a recluse. With him gone, one more reason for traditional rock radio was gone as well.

Don McLean had written "American Pie" about the day Buddy Holly was killed, the day the music died. Rock had risen phoenixlike from those ashes, but it was questionable if, without its king, it could be resurrected from the ruins of what it had become. The vitality seemed to be gone.

When a party is over, there's no getting the gaiety back. Try as the life of the party might, everybody's too tired to have fun and the feast is beginning to look like leftovers. That's where I found myself at the end of 1977—looking at rock 'n' roll's leftovers and trying to find the inspiration to be the life of the party for a while longer.

Jodie's antiques shop was going great guns. Whenever I could fudge a reason for being away from the station, we'd take off to the farm towns around the city to find collectible mementos of a simpler time. Refinishing furniture seemed far more meaningful to me than plugging Shaun Cassidy's sad imitation of the Crystals' "Da Doo Ron Ron." Soon I was looking for more than spatterware bowls and old advertising signs in the country. I was looking for a radio station I could own. There's not a jock who's been on the air for more than a few months who hasn't harbored the dream of one day owning a station. Since NYU I'd not only had that dream, but, as it was with my dream of being a radio star, I felt that my dream was my destiny.

Being newly consumed with turning my station-owner destiny into a reality told me something. I no longer was paying attention to what I was doing on the air. I had always vowed I'd give up being on the air if it ever became mechanical. I was just a step away from doing my show on automatic pilot. Facing my waning interest in being a full-time city radio personality was one thing. Initiating the end was another. Actually, the initiation didn't come from me. Youthful arrogance was something I knew about in connection with radio. Hadn't I had it in spades? Hadn't I witnessed it in countless others—sometimes with successful results, sometimes not? Still, the youthful arrogance of one Bob Pittman, maybe the fourth or fifth program director to be brought in by a nervous WNBC trying desperately to find a formula for successful AM rock radio when FM had all the formulas, was a shock.

With about three months to run on my three-year contract, young Mr. Pittman invited me to lunch. "Bruce, you don't need this anymore," he said, eyeing his meal with interest. "You've made your money. You've made your mark. Leave it to the younger guys." I didn't wait to find out the terms of my next contract. I tendered my resignation, effective at the end of the three years I'd signed up for, making it clear that my last broadcast would be simply a show like any other—no fanfare departure this time. Classic New York AM radio had left long ago—there was no big deal to be made about leaving it.

And so it ended. Seventeen years on New York radio. If I had done an average of 300 shows a year, I was going out with 5,100 shows among my souvenirs. I took with me the memories of these shows, the appearances, the mail, the promotions, the people who made it all possible—chairmen of boards, general managers, program directors, music librarians, concert promoters, stars, and everyone else behind the scenes who were the true virtuosos of the business. I'd met mayors and governors, starlets and directors, clowns and trapeze artists, painters and sculptors, singers and conductors. Rock 'n' roll had been my passport to the world. I'd been on the long journey with the people I truly loved—my listeners.

I had traveled in good company.

CHAPTER NINETEEN

Owned and Operated

In 1979 a great many people drove four-wheel-drive vehicles. Called rugged names like "Blazer," "Ramcharger," "Bronco," by their manufacturers, these tough machines were made for leaving life's toll roads and heading for the bushland, blazing your own trail as you went. Life, for many, had become too programmed. The wife, the two-and-a-third children, the car that got great mileage, the station wagon to use on car-pool days, the nurseries, preschools, and braces for the kids. A ski week in the winter if you were lucky and Christmas week at the in-laws', like it or not.

Rock 'n' roll's children had become miserably middle-aged and mired in an adulthood that didn't feel anything like their idealistic adolescence. The "me" decade had become the "what's wrong with me?" decade and therapists were doing nearly as well as lawyers. Not quite as well, however, since our country's irritability had resulted in a nationwide suing spree. We might have sued ourselves if we thought it would make us feel better.

To make matters worse, America was about to have its

second "gas crisis," a crisis of the spirit as much as of the pocketbook. The land of plenty felt like the land of penalty. We were penalized for everything from expecting a mortgage that was payable to wanting to go for a long Sunday drive.

The year 1978 had come to a strange close. In November we read of the mass suicide in Guyana. The dead were nearly all Americans, disciples of a cult leader named Rev. Jim Jones. Cyanide-laced Kool-Aid—the innocuous drink of our childhood, the smiling face on the glass pitcher—had been the hemlock of the humble followers of Rev. Jones. The Moonies, the Krishnas, the disciples of *est*, TM, Rolf, primal scream—our country's offspring seemed determined to go off the deep end. Had the proud individualists given way to the lemmings?

Still, the year ended on a reconciliatory note. President Carter announced that we were going to reestablish full diplomatic relations with China, a country most Americans had no idea of, if they even knew it still existed in the modern world. And so 1978 had become a new year, a year to be filled with international events that would give us hope one minute and heartache the next.

In 1979 we went from joy of a new partnership between Egypt and Israel to the unspeakable horror of having our fellow citizens taken hostage in a country we'd never paid any attention to. By the end of this year the vast majority of Americans would hear the name Khomeini at least once a day.

Musically, 1979 was a year of division. What sense could be made of the first two months of the decade's last twelve months when the charts had the Bee Gees at number one for two weeks, Chic's "Le Freak" at the top spot for three weeks, and Rod Stewart topping the heap for the last three weeks? The disco mirror era was still in full swing. Even rocker Stewart was gazing at himself. His hit asked us "Da Ya Think I'm Sexy?" We could only hope the next number-one song of 1979 would turn out to be prophetic when Gloria Gaynor sang "I Will Survive." By July of that year, the vast majority of radio listeners were united behind the slogan "Disco sucks."

It was the year Bob Dylan was born again, Bette Midler

haunted us as the Joplinesque Rose, and Sid Bernstein took out a twenty-thousand-dollar full-page ad in *The New York Times,* asking the Beatles to reunite at a benefit concert for the boat people. Nineteen seventy-nine. The year Chuck Berry went to prison for tax evasion. Who ever thought the government would expect Johnny B. Goode to pay taxes?

Come with me to March 1979:

Champagne glass in hand, as a prop and a barrier between me and all the well-wishers who want to pour for me, I'm squirming in a gray sports jacket that, regardless of the tailoring, will never fit my personality. Next to me is a thirty-year-old whom I now call my partner. His name is Bob Sillerman. After being introduced by Les and Nancy Marshak, we joined forces to find the radio station that would satisfy our mutual dream of owning a station. We're practically married, given all the ups and downs we've weathered together. We have found and bought a radio station. It's an AM-FM combo in Middletown, New York. It's housed in an old armory, a building the townspeople refer to as "the castle." There is no way I could feel more like a king than I do today. The castle is teeming with people. Local advertisers, politicians, and friends from far away have been invited to celebrate the day the "new WALL" goes on the air. At four o'clock today, surrounded by my flesh-and-blood family and this new family that I've taken on—the people who work at this station—I shall sit down at the console (officially "running the board" for the first time in my life, since small-market stations can't afford engineers) and kick off the beginning of a new radio station.

We've papered the area—basically Orange County, New York— with billboards. For a week or so the boards simply read YOU HAVE A VOICE IN YOUR FUTURE, ORANGE COUNTY. *Later they said,* THE VOICE IS COMING. *And today, miraculously, all the billboards have changed. They say* THE VOICE IS HERE. COUSIN BRUCIE ON 1340 AM. 4 PM MARCH 16.

We've been on the FCC files as wanting to own this station for six months. Waiting for them to OK the change in ownership hasn't exactly been a picnic for someone as impatient as I. Finally, last month the approval came through. That night we celebrated. The next day we walked into this building, faced the hopeful strangers, and told them they were going to have a ball. Since then, in just thirty days, we've revamped nearly everything about this place. I don't know about having a ball, but they've sure had an immersion. We were here till three this morning, filing records, wiring cartridge machines, even hanging artwork (my Dali is here) and window shades.

And so, blearily, I am about to go on the air as Cousin Owner. I have never had a day that felt like this. I am overwhelmed by a feeling of well-being. There is something so very peaceful about having attained this goal. No matter what happens after today, I will carry with me the sureness of this hour. The sureness is that all the nights in the windowless studios, all the days in the hot sun and freezing rain, all the times when I had to be Cousin Brucie without thinking about Bruce Morrow, all the moments that felt stolen because my six-night-a-week life simply had to come first, were all worth it. Now it seems they'd all pointed to today. "Today I am a man," a young boy is supposed to say when he comes of age. Henny Youngman didn't have a bar mitzvah until he was well into his sixties. "Today I am a boy," he said. That is how I feel. For twenty years I have been a grown-up kid. Today, though, I get to be just a kid. A kid whose wildest dream is coming true.

Now it's time to get in the studio and do my show. The 3:55 newscast has just begun. I'm going to open the show with my theme song. News director Al Larson is about to wrap up. I tug at my lapels, shift my weight, smile shakily, because what I think I'm going to do is cry. It's such a tiny studio. Jodie is here, and Les, Bob, and Jim Frey, the jock/copywriter whom I've named program director. Frankie Valli begins to sing "The Cousin Brucie Theme Song," as he has for so many, many times in my life. I open the mike at the end of the first stanza and say . . . "Yeeeeeeeeeeee!" Through the studio window I see people gaping at me. I look up and my friends in the studio are all weeping. So this is it. This is what it feels like when the love of something comes back as love for you. I have never felt this supremely excited and at peace before.

The jingle ends. The Cousin Brucie shout has ended. I open the mike and say, "Hi there, cousins, this is a special, special day . . ." I finish

*talking sooner than I expected. I'm too keyed up at the moment to
expect myself to turn thoughts into words. One more thing to say.
"OK, cousins, it's time to have some fun. I'm going to start the first
show on the first day of the new WALL as I've started every new
Cousin Brucie program in my life. It started at WINS and it's gone on
forever. Here's a legend for you. Chuck Berry. And "Maybelline"!*

By 1984, the Sillerman Morrow Broadcasting Group had
spread to eight radio stations in the Northeast and a television
station in Atlanta, and I was spreading myself too thin. Though
I'd moved my home base from WALL in Middletown, New
York, to WRAN-AM in Dover, New Jersey, in order to be closer
to the "normal" city life I was used to, things were anything
but normal. I made more appearances on interstates, chartered
twin engines, and jumbo jets than I did at home.

The peripatetic wanderings—from New Jersey to Pough-
keepsie, from there to Cape Cod, always going to a station or
coming from one, getting to Newark Airport with just seconds
to spare before folding myself into a 727 to Atlanta—wasn't a
life really. It was more of an itinerary.

Like many people for whom the dream comes true early and
is far better than one dared hope it would be, I spent some time
relearning what it takes to pay for the good fortune that was
mine. Owning one radio station was supposed to be a romp in
the country. Trying to run many more was an exercise in
insanity. While it obviously benefited me to be a part of a
growing broadcasting empire, I spent most of my time worrying and working ridiculous hours.

Every one of the radio stations had a format of its own, with
nuances geared to the locale and programming geared to the
target audiences. Atlanta was the real cruncher. Once every
twelve days it would take about fourteen hours in the TV
studio to record opening and closing tracks for two weeks'
worth of a taped daily show called *36 JV* (*36* being our UHF
channel and *JV* standing for Jukebox Video).

Bob Sillerman loved and had an enormous talent for business. I, on the other hand, felt like one of the S.O.B.'s I'd always railed against. My dream station was an enmeshing network now, and I was longing for the "simplicity" of settled city life. I was itchy to get back to the Big Apple. I needed to stroll the streets, to get a hot dog from my favorite guy on the corner of Fifty-fifth and Park, to go back to living in my home town. So we made the decision to sell all but the two properties in Northhampton, Massachusetts. Within a couple of months the deals were done and my heart and my stomach were starting to feel normal.

In 1978 Jodie and I had moved from Manhattan to Middletown. In 1981 we moved to one end of a pretty town called Mendham, New Jersey. In 1983 we went to the other end. In June 1984 we came back home. Home to Gotham, the Center of the World, Music Mecca, our turf. New York, New York. That first September back in the city took me back to NYU. This time I wasn't there as young Bruce Morrow. I was Cousin Professor. I looked out over that sea of eager faces and tried to guess. Did any of them have the flame, the burning need to do more than simply know about radio? Was there someone who would be too impatient to listen, someone who wanted to be talking, not to me or the class, but to the all-powerful faceless mass that is the unknown audience? Nothing would make me happier than to try to teach someone who was too impatient to listen to me.

One thing would make me happier, actually. And I had that too. Before I'd left WRAN, Joe McCoy, program director of New York's WCBS-FM had asked me to do a weekly Saturday night party show. I could only swing a monthly special, but when I got back to the city, I got back to the routine of being on every Saturday. Cousin Brucie was where he belonged—on the air on New York radio.

CHAPTER TWENTY

Cruisin' America

The Hyundai rode into America in 1986, a car from Korea, of all places. The cosmic *M*A*S*H* joke was being played on us for real. Lee Iacocca, the man who'd put Chrysler on its feet, was now busy putting the Statue of Liberty on safe footing and himself on the best-seller list. Audi, one of the darlings of the foreign-car converts, faced the horrifying possibility that its top-of-the-line model engaged itself into drive gear at breakneck, unstoppable speeds, killing drivers, passengers, standers-by. Nissan and Toyota battled for the title of most dominant Oriental car, while all the while the pickup continued to be the best-selling vehicle in America. We couldn't be summed up as a nation that was driven to drive any one car. BMWs in urban areas. Isuzus in exurbia. Chevrolet Cavaliers in suburbia. No wonder Korea felt the time was right to invade the U.S.A.

A country grown blasé about forays into space, now accustomed to the concept of using a spaceship to shuttle corporate payloads into the galaxy, we watched horrified as the

Challenger, intended to carry our first private citizen into space, instead carried Christa McAuliffe to death in the company of six of NASA's finest. Our pride and joy, our gilded space program, was now open to scrutiny and scandal and the kinds of headlines that we couldn't bear seeing about our last great fairy tale.

Ferdinand Marcos and the Shoe Queen were out of the Philippines, Baby and Mrs. Doc had fled Haiti. Terrorist bombs killed innocent citizens in Paris, London, Athens, West Berlin, Karachi, and Istanbul, and still we couldn't tell the Sandinistas from the Contras, or Iran from Iraq, without a scorecard. In November, an arms scandal stretching from Iran to Nicaragua with stops in Israel and, above all, Washington, D.C., began to unfold, an evil web spun, if not by our Teflon president himself, then certainly by the functionaries around him, who seemed to be running the nation anyway.

And what about that Statue of Liberty celebration? Liberty Weekend, U.S.A., 1986. We are nothing if not a country that can sit rapt in front of televised schmaltz. Despite the obscene rise in the number of our nation's homeless, we were ready to rally ''round the flag-waving lady in order to convince ourselves that this was still a country where the hungry, the poor, the huddled masses yearning to breathe free would find food, riches, the freedom to live and breathe in peace and prosperity. There were even two hundred Elvis imitators, an ironic touch from the nation that had once condemned Elvis as the gyrating devil seeking to shake loose the moral fiber of its young. A touch too showy? Perhaps, but after what we'd been through since the sixties, it took a lot of pizzazz to capture our imaginations and drag us back to the place where we still believed that America stood for the best in the human spirit: the conviction that all things are possible and that all possibilities are the birthright of all people. For a while on that Hollywood version of a July night, we did believe again.

In 1986, Halley's Comet went out of sight with a yawn. Corazon Aquino came in with a cheer. The Republicans lost control of Congress. The Mets won the World Series. A mixed bag of a year that gave me my most rose-colored view of the world to date.

Come with me to August 1986:

Wednesday evening on the subway uptown. The transit cops routinely stop me and say, "What are you doing down here, Cousin Brucie? You shouldn't be down in this zoo!"

"Just going to work," I sometimes reply. Or, "Hey, man, have you ever tried to get uptown in that traffic?"

There isn't a better way to get from home in the Village to Black Rock, the CBS building on Fifty-second and Sixth. Saturday nights are something else; there's no midtown traffic. I've been doing my Saturday party show on 101.1 FM for nearly two and a half years now, commuting by car, cab, limo, whatever seems right on the night, but weeknights are when the workers hold the city in their grip, a grip too tight to be broken by anything on four wheels on the streets. Besides, I'm curious about the adversity of the subway ride—the crush, the slightly devious look about things, the reality. I'm going uptown to talk to the city's real people; I'd better know what the city's real life is like.

Jeff Mazzei is still at the station when I get there. That's not surprising. Though my show doesn't start till 7:00, I never arrive past 5:30. Though Jeff, WCBS-FM's music director, is technically through at 5:00, he's not going anywhere. We talk about people in the business. I ask how Ron Lundy is doing. Ron's on WCBS-FM now. It's good to know he's here, although I rarely see him. That's fitting, in a way. When he had the show before Dan's on WABC, we ran into each other only at music meetings or "functions." Still, I feel a closeness with Ron that has nothing to do with getting together. He was a class act in those WABC days, a guy you could count on to keep the station sounding like a winner. He's doing the same thing here. And Harry is too. Yes, Harry Harrison has the WCBS-FM morning shift. I have come home. Jeff's got some record trivia for me to use on the show tonight. These days, people are studying the oldies as if they were a science. Bob Shannon, the jock with the shift before mine, has co-written a book called Behind the Hits, *talking about all the little-known facts about recorded music. Norm N. Nite, former WNBC jock and another WCBS-FM colleague, has written several volumes on rock, each titled* Rock On, *each labeled* The Illustrated Encyclopedia of Rock 'n' Roll. *He also has developed a rock data base software package. Bookstore shelves are crowded with authorized and unauthorized star bios—from the beautifully literate best seller* I, Tina *to Albert Goldman's* Elvis *exposé. Pulp about Springsteen and Elton John, and the various Rolling Stone anthologies and encyclopedias— rock is a subject of study now, thought of as a serious cultural and sociological phenomenon, not a trivial musical fad for the acne army. And, yes, I'm working on my own book. Brucie Meyerowitz writes a book—Mrs. Flink won't believe it. Rock has become entirely respectable now that it has enough of a past.*

Tonight's business is how that past connects with the present. Every Wednesday, I count down the top fifteen songs in the New York area. Those songs are interspersed with the top fifteen from one date throughout the years of rock history. I like being involved and identified with the current stuff, and it's the ultimate luxury for me to be able to blend the old and the new. It's also eerily appropriate, in view of what the phones tell me:

"Hi. This is Cousin Brucie. Who's this?"

"This is Bill Connelly from Queens, Cousin Brucie. It's great hearing you on the air. Like old times."

"Thanks, Cousin Bill. You like the oldies, huh?"

"Love 'em. My wife and I used to go on dates in my old Chevy convertible and listen to you on the radio. We listen to your Saturday show and talk about the good old days. My kids love the oldies too— and they love you. Listen, would you talk to my daughter JoAnne. She's a big fan . . ."

Of course I'll talk to his daughter JoAnne. Just as every week I talk to the kids of the kids who used to come to Palisades Park, and the grandchildren of the people who used to yell at their kids for keeping the radio on too late at night, and the forty-year-olds who are working late on Wall Street thinking about those days on the beach when the only time that was important was Chime Time on WABC. I've been hanging out with these people since 1960.

* * *

WABC to WNBC to WCBS. I've been sought by all three of the country's radio networks. I've given each of them a part of myself and a time of my life. New York City was the place where I could have access to those networks and now one of them is going to send me out across the country. RadioRadio, the CBS syndication network, has developed a new show called Cruisin' America, *starring Bruce "Cousin Brucie" Morrow.*

The first taping of Cruisin' America *was done in L.A. I hadn't been out there since the ill-fated filming of Robert Stigwood's* Sgt. Pepper *lemon, but L.A. was still L.A. Jodie and I were treated like royalty, as only the Left Coast can overdo it. In the studio, Ron Cutler, producer and creator of* Cruisin', *and Frank Murphy, RadioRadio's V.P. of programming, sat outside my soundproof booth, serious, pondering the large issues of radio syndication. On my side of the glass, I kept it light, waving, grinning (Deli Wars, anyone?). They laughed. Radio may be business, but it isn't serious business. The engineer took a voice level and then cued me to roll:*

> *"Hi there! This is your Cousin Brucie, cruisin' America on a highway paved with gold: golden memories and golden oldies. Each week, our three-hour cruise takes us back to where it all happened, with the people who made it all happen . . ."*

Yes, this radio magazine show is a weekly convertible ride around the nation when the music was young. The listeners can come with me to high school reunions in North Dakota and Galveston. We'll go back to Woodstock. We'll hear the first time the Dave Clark Five performed in the States and watch Bobby Rydell performing on the steel pier long before gambling came to Atlantic City. These features will be recreations, tapestries woven from the threads I've kept carefully stored in my memory. There are also to be interviews with the pioneers of rock, reflections on the early days of a musical form that no one expected to have later ones. I remember being about thirteen years old and hearing that everything that was ever said in the history of the world was still floating in space. With Cruisin' America, *I'm going to be the Catcher in the Sky, pulling in the words and music of the past thirty or so years, my entire adulthood—my and my country's extended youth. I can think of no more fitting role for myself.*

Is radio anybody's friend anymore? Does the blockbuster advance sale of the Springsteen live collection mean that rock is alive and well? Can the old AM sound make a comeback? And what about the morning-zoo format that the country has embraced, kind of off-color wake-up fare—is that here to stay? People ask me these questions and I give them my opinions. Yes, radio is a friend to some, but the friendship hasn't been tended in years. No, the Springsteen album doesn't indicate much except how powerful marketing has gotten, although Springsteen himself signifies the power of love—the love of the idiom called rock 'n' roll and how the obvious sincerity of that guy's love has made him one of contemporary rock's great troubadours. The old AM will never come back, but personality radio . . . yes, yes, that can come back. In fact, that morning-zoo stuff is an indication that people want personalities, not mechanics, on their radios. Even Howard Stern, who broadcasts in living off-color (in the mornings, yet—the Don Imuses of America have made morning the territory of the terrors), is a kind of throwback to personality radio—although I feel his shock-shlock schtick is not his real personality. I give the opinions because I'm asked to; it pleases me that I'm asked. Somewhere along the line the zany guy called Cousin became respectable.

I was once one of the reckless rocket cowboys flying by the seat of my pants. Now I'm cruisin' America talking about how it was and what it means. The reasons why I was able to be the former and why I can be doing the latter are the same. People are listening. The kids, the kids of the kids, the parents of the kids, the critics of the kids' music, and the creators of it. People listen because somewhere along the line, Top Forty radio became the closest thing we ever had to a national personality. Rock 'n' roll became the nearest thing we've ever had to an American voice. The testing just may be over. Indeed, rock 'n' roll does seem to be here to stay, and finally I can believe I am too.

THE BIG

M

BRUCE MORROW FAN CLUB

_____

MEMBER
_____
CHAPTER PRESIDENT
The "cousin" named on this card shall receive all privileges of a
member in good standing of the Bruce Morrow National Fan Club.

_____

THE BIG "M"